THE GLASS OF FORM

MIRRORING STRUCTURES FROM CHAUCER TO SKELTON

THE GLASS OF FORM

MIRRORING STRUCTURES FROM CHAUCER TO SKELTON

Anna Torti

D. S. BREWER

First published 1991 by D. S. Brewer, Cambridge

D. S. Brewer is an imprint of Boydell & Brewer Ltd
PO Box 9, Woodbridge, Suffolk IP12 3DF
and of Boydell & Brewer Inc.
PO Box 41026, Rochester, NY 14604, USA

ISBN 0 85991 313 9

British Library Cataloguing in Publication Data
Torti, Anna
The glass of form : mirroring structures from Chaucer to Skelton.
1. English Poetry. Imagery
I. Title
821.209
ISBN 0–85991–313–9

Library of Congress Cataloging-in-Publication Data
Torti, Anna.
The glass of form : mirroring structures from Chaucer to Skelton / Anna Torti.
p. cm.
Included bibliographical references and index.
ISBN 0–85991–313–9 (alk. paper)
1. English poetry – Middle English, 1100–1500 – History and criticism. 2. Mirrors in literature. 3. Chaucer, Geoffrey, d. 1400. Troilus and Criseyde. 4. Lydgate, John, 1370?–1451? Temple of glas. 5. Hoccleve, Thomas, 1370?–1450? Regement of princes. 6. Skelton, John, 1460?–1529 – Criticism and interpretation.
I. Title.
PR317.M57T67 1991
821'.20915–dc20 90–25686

This publication is printed on acid-free paper

Printed in Great Britain by
Woolnough Bookbinding Ltd, Irthlingborough, Northants

CONTENTS

To my mother
and to the memory of my father

PREFACE

This book originated from my interest in the often neglected fifteenth-century narrative. I began studying John Lydgate's *Temple of Glas* while I was teaching late medieval poetry at the University of Perugia in 1984 and I soon realized the importance of the mirror metaphor in the work of Lydgate and his contemporaries. The reasons for the fascination the mirror exerted on these poets are several, but two can be singled out: the analogical element in the mirror metaphor, which combines with the allegorical mode, and the ethical function attributed to poetry. Furthermore, fifteenth-century poets, who are reductively called Chaucerians, offer an interesting example of the ambivalence of the metaphor under discussion. On the one hand they clearly imitate Chaucer and their poetry represents a reflection (passive) of his works, on the other hand they try to give in their poems a new image (active) as far as form and content are concerned. The para-Shakespearean title of the book alludes to their use of mirroring structures: of course I take form in the modern sense of the term.

Like the Chaucerians, I too became fascinated by mirrors. The subject so intrigued me that I tried to analyse some of the various aspects of the metaphor in late medieval poetry. Vinge, Baltrušaitis, Grabes, and Lacan were my first critical guides in this investigation. Afterwards I necessarily turned to the two archetypical sources for the metaphor: Paul's Epistles to the Corinthians and the myth of Narcissus in Book III of Ovid's *Metamorphoses*.

To emphasize the role of the pagan and Christian archetypes at work in the poems under scrutiny, I decided to offer a detailed analysis of the constituent elements of the metaphor in the Introduction to this book. Discussions with Derek Brewer on the exploitation of the metaphor by Chaucer encouraged me to examine Chaucer's use of the concept of the mirror, and my first chapter is in fact on *Troilus and Criseyde*. The following chapter, on Lydgate, has benefited from the 'psychoanalytical' support of Sergio Rufini, while the study of Hoccleve's *Regement* was made easier by John Burrow's work on this poet. John Scattergood's edition of Skelton's *English Poems* and his criticism have helped a great deal in the writing of my last chapter.

Without the warm encouragement and the valuable suggestions of my 'mirours', Piero Boitani and Jill Mann, who have read the entire manuscript, this book would not have seen the light. I should also like to thank my students in Perugia who patiently backed my mirror obsession, and all the friends with whom I discussed my ideas at various stages of my research. I am particularly grateful to Richard Beadle, David Benson, Evelyn Bradshaw, Francesco Calvo, Douglas Gray, Nicholas Havely, Anthony Johnson, Giulio Lepschy, Francesca Montesperelli, Derek Pearsall, Stefania Piccinato, Marinella Salari, Howard Schless, E. G. Stanley, A. C. Spearing, and Barry Windeatt. The responsibility for all the errors and faults in the book is of course mine. Finally, my debt to my husband and son cannot be measured in words.

Parts of the book have been published in different form elsewhere. I am therefore grateful to Gunter Narr Verlag, to *Poetica* (Tokyo), and to *Textus* (Genoa), for permission to reprint, with revisions, material they have published.

This book is dedicated to my mother and to the memory of my father, both together 'ensaumples, for wele or for wo, / For ioy, turment, or for aduersite'.

Anna Torti
Spello, November 1989

NOTE ON TEXTS AND TRANSLATIONS

The classics are quoted from the Loeb Library unless otherwise specified. All other editions are given in the notes.

Introduction: The Mirror Metaphor in Medieval English Literature

Medieval writers made extensive reference to mirrors both literally and metaphorically.[1] A great number of works have *mirror* or *speculum* in their titles, thus pointing to their characteristics of compendium, summa, general view of the world. In this category we find narrative works such as the *Speculum Stultorum* and encyclopedic works such as Vincent of Beauvais' *Speculum Maius*, with its further subdivision into *Speculum Naturale*, *Speculum Historiale*, and *Speculum Doctrinale*. To function as a mirror a work of art does not have to be called *mirror* or *speculum*, since the didactic element is always prominent in a medieval author. Along with more general works showing the various aspects of the real world and aiming at the discovery of the ideal world of which society is a lower mirror, medieval literature is rich in the production of manuals for man to use as exemplary mirrors.

From both such general and individual mirrors we draw the ultimate meaning of the mirror metaphor, which is based on the same analogical element that permeates medieval culture. The mirror has in fact a double function: it is both positive and negative in showing us what we should be and what we are. This fundamental analogy goes back to Genesis 1: 26, where God, mirror of all Creation, creates man in His image and likeness. As man is similar to and different from God, so is

[1] On mirrors in general, see J. Baltrušaitis, *Le Miroir* (Paris, 1978), and more recently the interesting catalogue, *Lo Specchio e il Doppio. Dallo stagno di Narciso allo schermo televisivo*, edited by G. Macchi and M. Vitale (Milan, 1987) for the exhibition held in Turin (24 June – 11 October, 1987); see also B. Goldberg, *The Mirror and Man* (Charlottesville, 1985), especially chapters 7 and 8. The literary uses of the metaphor in England from the thirteenth to the seventeenth century are discussed in H. Grabes, *The Mutable Glass. Mirror Imagery in Titles and Texts of the Middle Ages and the English Renaissance*, trans. G. Collier (Cambridge, 1982); the ambivalence of the mirror metaphor is analysed in F. Goldin, *The Mirror of Narcissus in the Courtly Love Lyric* (Ithaca, N.Y., 1967). On allegory and mirror as literary modes in the Middle Ages, see J. I. Wimsatt, *Allegory and Mirror. Tradition and Structure in Middle English Literature* (New York, 1970), pp. 22–42, 137–62.

the image reflected in and by the mirror in relation to the real thing of which it is a 'similar copy'.

In the mirror-image relationship, the mirror has the active role as the means by which the ideal is seen in a transient image. That image is therefore both to be praised for its similarity to the ideal, and to be treated with caution on account of its temporariness. The mirror's essentially ambivalent role, of reflecting appearances (sensible phenomena) and of revealing an intimation of the invisible, the divine, behind them, has to be borne in mind for an understanding of the frequent use of the mirror metaphor in literature.

As I have stressed above, in medieval literature the metaphor works in various direct and indirect ways, by openly presenting itself in the title or by covertly structuring the narrative, while always implying the basic analogical assumption. The mirror metaphor thus combines with the all-pervading medieval literary mode, that of allegory, equally founded on analogy. Allegory establishes a kind of mirror-relationship between the literal and the secondary (allegorical, tropological, anagogical) levels of discourse, thus revealing the inseparable connection between the world of phenomena and the universal truths which lie behind. Writing allegory is a way of functioning as the mirror does: allegorical narrative relates a fictive story and at the same time is strongly conscious of the story as a fiction of which the validity depends on the non-fictional, *true* relationship with the ideal, with God's Word.

The reasons for the success of the metaphor, as will be shown later, are to be found in the Neoplatonic world-picture with its related doctrine of correspondences, in the ethical function attached to medieval literature, and in the renewed interest in the glass mirror as a domestic article. In the following pages I shall try to deal with the various, often opposed elements of the metaphor, by analysing its major sources.

To return to the mirror's analogical basis, an immediate consequence is to be inferred in so far as the reflected image may be neither completely positive nor entirely negative. If the mirror's capacity consists in sending back an image which is transient yet reminiscent of its link with the subject, then the metaphor's outcome in literature conveys the two connotations. A poem such as *Pearl* is a mirror of the ideal, of what will happen in the afterlife, and at the same time it shows man's difficulty in understanding ultimate truths. The play *Magnyfycence* is a mirror of what the ruler should avoid, given the utter insecurity of this world, but it also implies hope in the final salvation of Magnyfycence himself.

In this work, I shall examine the various aspects of the metaphor, and in particular focus on the mirror structure informing the poems under examination. Not only are my examples mirrors *of* and *for* some categories of mankind, but also mirror-structured literary works through the use of parallelism, chiasmus, and other rhetorical devices. It is therefore possible to see the metaphor at work at the deep level of the formal organization of late medieval narrative.

The mirror has fascinated man in every age, as many works on the subject in literature and in art witness. The myth of Perseus and Medusa, the episode of Rinaldo's bewitching by Armida in Tasso's *Jerusalem Delivered*, the symbolic connection with the purity of the Virgin Mary and with the beauty of Venus, and the opposite symbolic meanings of Wisdom and Vanitas as shown in the mirror are but a few examples of the pervasiveness of the metaphor. Nevertheless to account for its wide diffusion in the Middle Ages and later, two examples – one from Christianity and the other from the pagan world – must be singled out: Paul's reference to the mirror in the Epistles to the Corinthians, and the myth of Narcissus as narrated in the *Metamorphoses*.

The biblical Book of Wisdom defines wisdom in the following terms:

> Candor est enim lucis aeternae,
> Et speculum sine macula Dei maiestatis,
> Et imago bonitatis illius.
>
> (For she is the brightness of eternal light,
> and the unspotted mirror of God's majesty,
> and the image of his goodness; Wisdom 7: 26.)[2]

This verse condenses the three characteristics related to the mirror metaphor so widely exploited by the medieval *auctores*: light, mirror, and image. As they define absolute wisdom, the three elements are to be interpreted positively; they are exempt from those human limitations to which Paul refers in his Epistles to the Corinthians:

> Videmus nunc per speculum in aenigmate: tunc autem facie ad

[2] The edition of the Bible used in the Introduction and throughout the book is the following: *Biblia Vulgata*, eds. A. Colunga and L. Turrado, 6th edn. (Madrid, 1982). The English translation is the Douay-Rheims version: *The Holy Bible, Translated from the Latin Vulgate* (Rockford, Ill., 1971). I shall specify when I use the King James version and *The New English Bible with the Apocrypha* (Oxford and Cambridge, 1970).

faciem. Nunc cognosco ex parte: tunc autem cognoscam sicut et cognitus sum.

(We see now through a glass in a dark manner: but then face to face. Now I know in part; but then I shall know even as I am known; I Cor. 13: 12.)

Nos vero omnes, revelata facie gloriam Domini speculantes, in eandem imaginem transformamur a claritate in claritatem, tamquam a Domini Spiritu.

(But we all beholding the glory of the Lord with open face, are transformed into the same image from glory to glory, as by the Spirit of the Lord; II Cor. 3: 18.)

From Genesis 1: 26 on ('Faciamus hominem ad imaginem et similitudinem nostram' – Let us make man to our image and likeness) created man is linked to God in a mirror relationship: man is made in God's image and likeness. It can easily be understood how knowledge based on the mediation of a mirror lends itself to various interpretations which depend on the very nature of the medium. At the heart of the cognitive relationship is the mirror, which of necessity refers back to a source in order to reflect an image – and this image is in turn directed towards a particular viewer. The mirror therefore has a double but opposite function: positive in the sense that it provides an image of what we ought to be, and negative in that it displays transitory, and consequently vain images.

In I Corinthians it seems to be Paul's intention to stress at least the imperfection – if not the negative quality – of human vision; in II Corinthians, however, he succeeds in reconciling the dichotomy between absolute wisdom and the knowledge conceded to natural man precisely by exploiting the positive value of the mirror metaphor. By reflecting God's splendour as in a mirror man changes himself into the very image he reflects: from the prophetic vision of the man-God relationship of the First Epistle we attain the eschatological perfection of man's seeing God face to face.[3] In his two Epistles Paul makes typologi-

[3] Paul's use of the mirror metaphor in I Corinthians in an epistemological context is discussed by R. Mortley, 'The Mirror and I Cor. 13, 12 in the Epistemology of Clement of Alexandria', *Vigiliae Christianae* 30 (1976) 109–20, by analysing Clement's exegesis of the Pauline Epistle. As N. Hugedé in *La métaphore du miroir dans les Epîtres de Saint Paul aux Corinthiens* (Neuchâtel/Paris, 1957), pp. 17ff., has

cal reference[4] to the constituent elements of the mirror metaphor summed up in the definition found in Sapientia: *candor* appears as *claritate*, *speculum* is repeated along with *speculantes*, *imago* is present as *imaginem*.

Whereas *speculum* and *imago*, since they refer to Divine Wisdom, seem synonymous in the Old Testament, Paul makes a distinction between the mediating function of the *speculum* when this is viewed in its material and imperfect nature, and its ameliorating function when it displays an image of the splendour of our Lord in which man can see his own likeness. The *imaginem* of the Second Epistle is thus a reflection of divine glory (this connotation is strengthened by the participle *speculantes*), and at the same time a new image that takes form gradually, as little by little man continues to grow in God's image and likeness. The Holy Ghost makes possible this transition from obscurity (*in aenigmate*) to clarity (*facie ad faciem*), from what we are to what we ought to be. Paul's sophisticated distinction – which in the final analysis refers back to the fundamental difference between natural and spiritual man – is based on the analogy with which the mirror provides us. This analogy is well described by John Chrysostom in the parable of the barber: the mirror gives back our image as it is, and we compare the information with our ideal image. If there is a discrepancy between the two 'images', it is up to the barber to make them correspond by giving us a different haircut or trim.[5]

Epistemologically, Paul's Epistles represent the two basic stages of knowledge: imperfect human knowledge (*videmus*, *cognosco ex parte*), and complete knowledge in the afterlife (*cognoscam sicut et cognitus*

pointed out, the difference between an imperfect and a 'face to face' vision of God is evident in I Corinthians. Problems arise in II Cor. 3: 18, where the Greek verb *katoptrizomenoi* could be translated either simply 'beholding' (Douay-Rheims) and 'beholding as in a glass' (King James version), or 'we reflect as in a mirror' (New Bible) with the implied emphasis on the negative meaning in one case and on the positive meaning of the metaphor in the other case. The active and passive aspects of the mirror metaphor are also discussed by P. Demiéville, 'Le miroir spirituel', *Sinologica* 1 (1948) 112–37.

4 The figural or typlogical approach *in* and *to* the Bible and to medieval literature is first discussed in Auerbach's exemplary essay 'Figura', trans. R. Manheim, in E. Auerbach, *Scenes from the Drama of European Literature* (New York, 1959). The importance of this method is also stressed, among others, by E. Salter, 'Medieval Poetry and the Figural View of Reality', *Proceedings of the British Academy* 54 (1968) 73–92, and by F. Kermode, *The Genesis of Secrecy. On the Interpretation of Narrative* (Cambridge, Mass., 1979), especially ch. V.

5 The parable is quoted in Grabes, *The Mutable Glass*, pp. 140–1.

sum). In addition to echoing the Book of Wisdom and other *loci* of the Old Testament, Paul's words are thus also the product of a philosophical tradition that goes back to Plato's treatment of the question of knowledge in *I Alcibiades*.

Here, according to Socrates, man's knowledge of the divine is acquired through self-knowledge. When one man looks at another, his face is reflected in the other's eye, or, more precisely, in the pupil – the part that contains the organ of sight. Similarly, when the noblest part of a man – his soul – seeks self-knowledge, it looks to that part of itself where lies wisdom, a virtue that is the image of God. And just as mirrors are clearer than the reflecting eye, so God is the best and clearest mirror of the best part of the soul. Whoever looks and recognizes the divine in his soul knows himself.[6]

It would seem that Athanasius in the *Contra Gentes* was the first to introduce the idea of the soul as a mirror – capable, when pure, of reflecting God's image – into Christian thought.[7] The metaphor is also frequently used by Augustine – for example, in *De Trinitate*, and in *De Vera Religione* – where self-knowledge is seen as a means to know God: 'Noli foras ire, in te ipsum redi: in interiore homine habitat veritas' (Do not roam abroad, return unto thyself. Truth dwells in the inner man; XXXIX, 72). When the Fathers of the Church state that the soul reflects the image of God, they make use of an analogy to explain that the soul *is* the image of God. The mirror image really exists because – according to the Greeks – when we see an image in a mirror, the rays from the eye meet with those projected by the visible object, so forming the image we see on the mirror's surface. Thus self-knowledge – that is, knowledge of one's soul – is tantamount to knowledge of God, because God created the soul to reflect His image. In this way, by means of the mirror metaphor, the soul is considered as God's true image, even though it

[6] See *I Alcibiades* 133 a–c. Part of the passage (in particular, the idea that the soul is an image of God) may be a Neoplatonic interpolation. On the influence of the Platonic idea of the mirror on Christianity, see J. Pépin, *Idées grecques sur l'homme et sur Dieu* (Paris, 1971), and Mortley's 'The Mirror and I Cor.'. The difference between the Neoplatonic meaning of the mirror and the Christian senses is discussed by Sr. R. Bradley, 'The Speculum Image in Medieval Mystical Writers', in M. Glasscoe, ed., *The Medieval Mystical Tradition in England* (Cambridge/Woodbridge, 1984), pp. 9–27, who maintains that the influence of Platonism on the mystics is minimal.

[7] See A. Louth, *The Origins of the Christian Mystical Tradition. From Plato to Denys* (Oxford, 1981), who connects Athanasius' idea to the Greek theory of light found in an appendix to the *Timaeus* (46 a–c), pp. 78–80.

depends on God Himself; it is therefore affirmed that the divine image in the soul can be perceived by means of self-knowledge.[8]

To come back to Paul, if we accept an epistemological interpretation of the parts concerning the mirror in the two Epistles to the Corinthians, we see that he uses the metaphor positively in both cases: it is only time that changes, since *now* we see darkly and *then* we shall see clearly. If *speculatio* (and *contemplatio*) are the Latin for the Greek *theoria*, then *speculatio* as a subdivision of *theoria* means the search for knowledge for its own sake, a search which has as its ultimate aim the knowledge of God.[9] For a man to attain knowledge by means of the *speculum* he must pass through its various stages in order to reach the whole from the part, at which point he becomes the image reflected by his soul. In I Corinthians the Greek is translated with *videmus per speculum* (*we see through a glass*) and in II Corinthians with *speculantes* (*beholding*), but it remains clear that Paul is concerned with the question of knowledge, since knowledge is none other than reflection and contemplation – as Socrates also teaches us.[10]

If Paul represents the prime example of the Christian use of the mirror metaphor, Narcissus is the most relevant pagan embodiment of the same metaphor. The myth which Ovid recounts in *Metamorphoses* III – and which was moralized by medieval mythographers – expresses man's innate desire for knowledge.[11] Narcissus sees his reflection in the spring,

8 On the association of self-knowledge with God from Plato to medieval exegesis, see, apart from P. Courcelle's monumental *Connaîs-toi toi-même de Socrate à Saint Bernard* (Paris, 1974–75), H. Leisegang, 'La connaissance de Dieu au miroir de l'âme et de la nature', *Revue d'histoire et de philosophie religieuses* 2 (1937) 145–71, pp. 150ff.; E. G. Wilkins, *The Delphic Maxims in Literature* (Chicago, 1929), ch. V; and the interesting survey of the problem by J. A. W. Bennett, '*Nosce te ipsum*: Some Medieval and Modern Interpretations', in J. A. W. Bennett, *The Humane Medievalist and other Essays in English Literature and Learning, from Chaucer to Eliot*, ed. P. Boitani (Rome, 1982), pp. 135–72.

9 On the different meaning of the term 'speculation' in scholastic and post-Cartesian philosophy, see R. Gasché, *The Tain of the Mirror. Derrida and the Philosophy of Reflection* (Cambridge, Mass., and London, 1986), pp. 42ff.

10 The Latin *speculantes* in II Corinthians is also translated, in the New English Bible, as *reflect as in a mirror*. *Reflectere* means to send back, to reflect, to meditate. Such a translation gives support to the centrality of knowledge in Paul.

11 The best account of the Narcissus theme in literature is still L. Vinge, *The Narcissus Theme in Western European Literature up to the Early Nineteenth Century*, trans. R. Dewsnap, N. Reeves (Lund, 1967), to which the present analysis owes a great deal. See also Goldin's *Mirror of Narcissus*, Introduction; R. Tuve, *Allegorical Imagery* (Princeton, 1966), pp. 36, 41, 45, 262; D. W. Robertson, Jr., *A Preface to Chaucer: Studies in Medieval Perspectives* (Princeton, 1962), pp. 93–4; A. D. Nuttall, 'Ovid's Narcissus and Shakespeare's Richard II: The Reflected Self', in C. Martindale, ed.,

but the sight of it proves fatal to him. The young man is 'visae correptus imagine formae' (carried away by the sight of the beautiful form he sees; 416, trans. F. J. Miller in the Loeb library), then 'spectat humi positus geminum, sua lumina, sidus' (prone on the ground, he gazes at his eyes, twin stars; 420) and 'cunctaque miratur, quibus est mirabilis ipse' (in short, he admires all the things for which he is himself admired; 424). By using a string of terms such as *visae*, *lumina*, and *miratur*, Ovid insists on the purely external nature of Narcissus' vision. The deceptive nature of his way of looking is stressed later on by 'Se cupit inprudens' (unwittingly he desires himself; 425); the charge of self-infatuation echoes with an inverse sense Tiresias' prophetic words ('Si se non noverit' – If he does not know himself; 348) when he made this the ominous condition to the happiness of a long life on earth. In reality, Narcissus does not at first understand, and is unaware that he is his own love-object; then comes the ironic realization that 'iste ego sum: sensi, nec me mea fallit imago' (Oh, I am he! I have felt it, I know now my own image; 463). Narcissus has a palpable, contingent, material experience – *sensi* – and his image both does and does not deceive him. The paradox of Narcissus' condition, which the ambiguity of *imago* alludes to, is synthesized in the entropy expressed in the two hexameters,

> quod cupio, mecum est: inopem me copia fecit.
> o utinam a nostro secedere corpore possem!
>
> (What I desire, I have; the very abundance of my riches beggars me. Oh, that I might be parted from my own body; 466–7.)

The present tense *cupio* is coupled with the fatal *fecit*; the excess of *mecum* and *copia* is balanced against the central, realistic *inopem*. The one is seen to be deceptively two, as the possessive plural *nostro* associated with the first person singular *possem* shows, and nothing now remains for Narcissus but the illusory hope of wrenching himself away from his own self. But since this is not possible, the self not allowing of separation, only death, the final annihilation, offers a way of escape from this paradox. 'Nunc duo concordes anima moriemur in una' (but as it is, we two shall die together in one breath; 473). In this way the divided identity is made one again (*concordes*) in the same spirit.

Ovid Renewed (Cambridge, 1988), pp. 137–50. On Echo, see L. Ritter Santini, 'La favola di Eco: *Langue et parole*', in L. R. Santini and E. Raimondi, eds., *Retorica e critica letteraria* (Bologna, 1978), pp. 151–78.

In this analysis of the myth of Narcissus we cannot, of course, forget its other mirror aspect, the story of Echo. Narcissus represents the *imago formae*, Echo an *imago vocis*, able to do nothing more than to send back – *re-flectere* – others' voices. The theme of spatial reflection in the pool is anticipated by the theme of auditory reflection represented by Echo (*vocalis nymphe* – a vocal nymph – 357; *resonabilis Echo* – resounding Echo – 358). Fated by Juno to repeat final words, the nymph pleads her love of Narcissus with 'Sit tibi copia nostri' (I give you power over me; 392), which is an abbreviated version, rich in erotic connotations, of Narcissus' spurning refusal 'Ante . . . emoriar, quam sit tibi copia nostri' (May I die before I give you power over me; 391). There is a clear foreshadowing in the Echo episode of the terms that we will find at the end. Narcissus would rather die than yield to the nymph; but that *copia nostri* alludes to much more than sexual union with Echo: the allusion is to the image of himself, as one and also as two, which drives Narcissus to desperation and death.

The curse of one of the nymphs spurned by the young man ('sic amet ipse licet, sic non potiatur amato' – So may he himself love, and not gain the thing he loves; 405) is also added to Tiresias' terrible prophecy: self-knowledge is dangerous, because it implies aspiration towards the unattainable. The reflection of Narcissus in the water disappears, and with it his body: Echo can do no more than join in the mourning of the Dryads ('planxerunt dryades: plangentibus adsonat Echo' – the Dryads, too, lamented, and Echo gave back their sounds of woe; 507).

All that remains of Narcissus is a flower, and Echo has become a stone: the bond between the two bodies lies in Echo's voice, fated to remain silent unless in the presence of another voice. Echo must imitate, must ever be an image. According to Socrates, the soul can grasp the idea of the divine by means of self-knowledge, whereas for Ovid this idea remains unintelligible, since self-knowledge is not possible. Of the four stages of knowledge Plato speaks of (*Republic* VII), man can reach only the first: this stage is imagination (*eikasia*), by which isolated sense images are perceived. Echo was divided by Juno into body-stone and sound, and then reduced to sound only. Narcissus becomes more and more isolated and falls in love with his own image; and the entropy of this desire is resolved in death, in the unity of that *anima una* – perhaps the world soul, the model *par excellence* for the human soul, the place where the Same and the Different co-exist.[12]

12 See Plato's *Timaeus* 35 a–c.

Plotinus' reworking of the myth of Narcissus as the emblem of those who choose to love 'beautiful bodies', vain shadows, also lays stress on the mistakenness of sense-limited knowledge. According to Plotinus, man must be capable of turning his attention from copies, from vestiges and shadows, towards what lies behind them.[13] This reading is taken over by medieval writers such as John of Salisbury, Alexander Neckam, and Arnulf of Orléans who, in their rationalization of the myth, insist on the connection between self-love and earthly *vanitas*. Narcissus becomes either the emblem of those who refuse to submit to the power of love, or the archetype of those who love to excess, and his metamorphosis into a flower is justified by the allusion to the symbolism of the flower associated with man's pride and ambition from the Bible on.[14] The central issue is no longer self-knowledge and its risks – ultimately the annihilation wrought by death – as Ovid's reconstruction of the myth gave his readers to understand, but the recovery, in a negative sense, of an *exemplum* of pagan folly. Narcissus mistakes his own image for something different, and for this reason his impossible love is insane. The pool-mirror has now become the sign of a fatal confusion between illusion and reality.

We have noted that Plotinus uses the Narcissus myth to stress the vanity and the impermanence of worldly things; elsewhere, in the *Enneads*, however, he defines the soul as a mirror that displays the images of the intelligibles.[15] This apparent contradiction is resolved by the fact that the intelligibles are as if reflected in a mirror: either in the mind, where they remain as ideas, or in matter, where they form an illusory world of shadows. These shadows, vain and degraded in the chain of being though they may be, are a replica of the ideas, and it was on this conceptual basis that in his *Commentarium* Marsilio Ficino was induced to make a re-evaluation of worldly beauty as the image of spiritual beauty. For Ficino, Narcissus' error is thus a detour along the path of

13 Plotinus, 'On the Beautiful', *Enneads* I, 6.8 (8–12). See also Goldin, *The Mirror of Narcissus*, pp. 6–7.

14 On Narcissus as an *exemplum* of vainglory in the Middle Ages, see Vinge, *The Narcissus Theme*, ch. III; P. Boitani, *Chaucer and the Imaginary World of Fame* (Cambridge, 1984), pp. 98–100; J. Frappier, 'Variations sur le thème du miroir, de Bernard de Ventadour à Maurice Scève', *Cahiers de l'Association Internationale des Études Françaises* 11 (1959) 134–58, especially pp. 141–4.

15 *Enneads* I, 4.10. For an explanation of Plotinus' use of the mirror metaphor, see Sr. R. Bradley, 'Backgrounds of the Title *Speculum* in Medieval Literature', *Speculum* 29 (1954) 100–15, pp. 105–7, and R. Ferwerda, *La signification des images et des métaphores dans la pensée de Plotin* (Groningen, 1965), pp. 9–23, 123–31.

aspiration towards the beautiful. Narcissus has stopped at the shadow instead of aspiring to the beautiful in its highest form, that is, to God.[16]

The mirror is of course found very frequently in mythology, as in the story of Perseus' slaying of Medusa: Perseus used Athena's shield as a mirror in order to localize and slay the Gorgon without being turned into stone by her glance. This *mythos* bears close analogies to that of Narcissus, in that the Gorgon's eyes, with their power to turn men into stone, are used by Perseus to kill his enemies: they thus become instruments of death, just as Narcissus' eyes are when they prevent him from tearing himself free of the self-image in which he will find his death.[17]

This brief survey from Plato and the Bible to Ficino, in the course of which I have examined the two significant motifs – one Christian and one pagan – for the construction of the mirror metaphor, is offered as an illustration of the many-sided potential of the image in the Late Middle Ages from Chaucer to Skelton.[18]

The metaphor can be exploited in different ways. On the one hand the double value, passive/active, of the mirror image, and its ability to reflect in a positive or a negative way are apparent; on the other the epistemological problem connected with the exploitation of the metaphor in Paul and Ovid should be taken into account. It is correct to insist, as some critics have done, on the imperfection of man's vision of God in Paul, but there still remains for the Christian – and in this case the medieval Christian – the eschatological motif of man's likeness to God in the afterlife as foretold by the prophets. The myth of Narcissus is splendidly evocative of the solitude and the psychological isolation of man, in that he disdains all contact with others, and his only words are in reply to a voice from which they return as echoes, but only in part,

16 On Marsilio Ficino's understanding of the myth of Narcissus as an illustration of the choice between material and spiritual beauty, see Vinge, *The Narcissus Theme*, pp. 123–7.

17 Cf. T. Siebers, *The Mirror of Medusa* (Berkeley, Los Angeles, London, 1983), pp. 11–14, 69.

18 The frequent use of Paul's mirror image in medieval theological and literary writings and the exploitation of the Narcissus theme in medieval poetry, mainly French, account for the prominence given to these two archetypes of the metaphor. Both instances are exemplary, the Pauline mirror showing the world's resemblance to and distance from God, and the Narcissus myth stressing the inadequacy of the image and the impossibility of going beyond the mirror. A. Fowler, in his review of Grabes, *The Mutable Glass*, after a brief survey of the Christian and pagan origins of the metaphor, rightly points out the necessity for a study of the relationship between the change in reciprocity of subject and object and the increasing number of mirror metaphors in Elizabethan poetry (A. Fowler, 'Through the Looking-glass', *Times Literary Supplement* – 19 August, 1983, p. 872).

and therefore with an altered meaning. The myth thus alludes to the impossibility of man's achieving any form of contact with the Other, because to do so would involve passing through self-knowledge, and this is shown to be dangerous. Self-knowledge, according to the Delphic maxim that Socrates explains to Alcibiades, is knowledge of the soul: Narcissus went no further than knowledge of the body, only on the point of death referring to the *anima una*. The question of knowledge in Narcissus is not, however, touched on in the Middle Ages; medieval writers are more interested in the illusoriness and the vanity of self-love suggested by the myth.

Medieval literature makes extensive use of the mirror metaphor, by considering the book itself as mirror to justify the rewriting of the Scriptures. In Augustine's *Enarratio in Psalmum, CIII*, the Sacred Scriptures act as mirror:

> Posuit tibi speculum Scripturam suam; legitur tibi: *Beati mundi corde, quoniam ipsi Deum uidebunt*. Speculum in hac lectione propositum est: uide si hoc es quod dixit: si nondum es, geme ut sis. Renuntiabit tibi speculum faciem tuam: sicut speculum non senties adulatorem, sic nec te palpes. Hoc tibi ostendit nitor ille quod es: uide quod es.
>
> (The mirror has set its writing before you; it is read to you: *Blessed are the pure in heart, for they shall see God*. The mirror is set forth in this reading; see whether you are what it has said. If you are not yet so, then groan, that you may become so. The mirror will disclose your face to you. As you will not see a flatterer in the mirror, so you will not cajole yourself. Its brightness will show you what you are: see what you are.)[19]

The Scriptures are therefore a corrective mirror: they show man what he should be – pure in heart – but also what he in fact is – a sinner capable of reforming himself. Just as the Bible, *the* Book, is the compendium of God's teachings for man, so in the Middle Ages books acted as corrective mirrors for man's moral improvement. This they were to achieve by making the reader compare himself continually with the ideal image which was always, by divine intervention, present in his consciousness. The mirror metaphor may take different forms in medieval literature,

19 (PL 32, 1338), quoted in Goldin, *The Mirror of Narcissus*, p. 5.

but, in a culture based on the analogical principle, it inevitably became central. Medieval authors, even though they do not give their works the title of *speculum*, feel themselves part of the universal divine design, in which their books are written for their didactic function. They are accurate in their realistic details, self-sufficient, and at the same time inextricably bound in time to the Book of God in which all is written.[20]

Allegory is a favourite literary mode in the Middle Ages in that it presents universal ideals somewhat obscured by realistic details. Allegory could be considered a kind of 'mirror-writing', since it aims at pointing to the ideal beyond the real or at showing the connection between the real and the ideal. If a total reciprocity exists between creature and Creator, man and God, particular and universal, object and subject, then the most appropriate form of writing is that based on allegory: or more precisely, to quote Auerbach, on the particular kind of allegory that is typology. Perhaps the most general definition of allegory is given by Isidore of Seville when he speaks of *alieniloquium*:[21] the poet says one thing and implies another. If this definition is relevant in terms of Platonic allegory – according to which the world of ideas is revealed in shadowy form in the visible world – it is not sufficient to explain the typological process, which holds that one thing does not only stand for another, but that it makes it a part of itself and gives it substance. The distance between God and the world is cancelled by the Incarnation, by the Word that became flesh. The typological way of writing thus offers the means not only of connecting man's destiny to world history, but above all of engaging the particular Christian reader in the process of redemption.[22] The answer to man's and the reader's search for his soul's salvation lies in Christ, who is both God and man. Christ becomes a mirror with which man must compare himself on his pilgrimage through a sinful life towards the afterlife.[23] The meaning of Paul's words is clear: to see by means of a mirror means to see a resemblance according to an

20 For a discussion of Scripture as mirror, see Goldin, *The Mirror of Narcissus*, pp. 8–13. For the metaphor of the world as a book, cf. E. R. Curtius, *European Literature and the Latin Middle Ages*, trans. W. R. Trask (New York, 1953), ch. 16, and Kermode, *The Genesis of Secrecy*, p. 121.

21 *Etymologiae* I, xxxvii, 22.

22 See A. C. Charity's comprehensive study of Christian typology: *Events and their Afterlife. The Dialectics of Christian Typology in the Bible and Dante* (Cambridge, 1966).

23 For a Christological interpretation of the idea of self-knowledge through the mirror in Clement of Alexandria, cf. Mortley, 'The Mirror and I Cor.', pp. 117–20.

analogical process which is valid both on the epistemological and the literary plane.

Thomas Aquinas used the metaphor of the mirror to suggest the similarity between things created and their universal forms. In the *De Veritate* he describes two different ways of regarding the mirror of God. The first way is to consider the divine mirror as an object in itself, but this only the heavenly host and the blessed can do; the second is to observe the universal forms of created things as they are reflected in the Divine Mind. God is a mirror capable of producing likenesses *without* a pre-existing object. If God is a *speculum superius*, man is a *speculum inferius*.[24]

Despite the imperfection of sin, man reflects the divine image, because God illumines the intellectual faculty of the human soul directly and thereby allows it a limited perception of truth. In the thirteenth century the conception of God as *speculum superius* is justified by its association with the metaphysics of light, whose major exponent was Robert Grosseteste.[25] Theories of light go back to their earliest appearance in Plato's *Republic*, where he insists that knowledge of eternal forms is acquired by a process analogous to the vision of the imperfect material world.[26] Augustine also deals with this theme and sees God as eternal light and the source of all other light. In the *De Trinitate* he speaks of three types of vision: corporeal, spiritual, and intellectual.[27] This terminology gives him the basis on which to elaborate the theory that man contains within himself the image of the Trinity. Grosseteste makes a synthesis of Augustinian Platonism and Aristotelian science,[28] and at-

24 *Quaestiones disputatae de veritate* q.12 a.6 ob.8. quoted by J. L. Miller, 'Three Mirrors of Dante's *Paradiso*', *University of Toronto Quarterly* 46 (1977) 263–79, pp. 270–1, who analyses the mirror of creation in Dante.

25 For a survey of medieval and Renaissance theories of light, see D. C. Lindberg, *Theories of Vision from Al-Kindi to Kepler* (Chicago and London, 1976), who has written extensively on the subject. On the medieval interest in optics, see W. Theisen, 'Euclid's *Optics* in the Medieval Curriculum', *Archives internationales d'histoire des sciences* 32 (1982) 159–76. On 15th century optics as an important stage in the development of optics from medieval to modern science, cf. G. Rosińska, 'Fifteenth-Century Optics between Medieval and Modern Science', *Studia Copernicana* 24 (Warsaw, 1986).

26 On Plato's theory of knowledge, cf. P. Louis, *Les métaphores de Platon* (Paris, 1945), especially ch. III.

27 *De Trinitate* XI, 3–5.

28 On Grosseteste's important role in medieval optics, see A. C. Crombie, *Robert Grosseteste and the Origins of Experimental Science, 1100–1700* (Oxford, 1953); B. S. Eastwood, 'Mediaeval Empiricism: The Case of Grosseteste's Optics', *Speculum* 43 (1968) 306–21; J. McEvoy, *The Philosophy of Robert Grosseteste* (Oxford, 1982).

tributes all the changes in the universe to the activity of the corporeal form (*lux*), the primal light which emanates from God and which has the ability to create forms in the Divine Mind or out of inchoate matter. The other type of light (*lumen*) is the reflected light visible in the material cosmos. The two types of light, while separate, are not, according to Grosseteste, opposed to each other.[29] Taking as their basic premise a correspondence between *lumen* in the material universe and *lux* in the spiritual cosmos, the metaphysical philosophers of light attribute the mirror metaphor to God.

The interest in optics and in the science of mirrors is very marked among the Franciscans and the Dominicans, and the thirteenth century sees the great syntheses of Roger Bacon, John Pecham and Witelo.[30] In spite of the wealth of distinguished works on optics and the various theories of sight, many questions remain unanswered. Are there separate rays? Are light and colour related phenomena? What relationship exists between *lumen* and *lux*? This brief review of the problems raised by optics, a science which was widely esteemed,[31] allows us to note another sequence of works that seems to lead to the widespread interest in mirrors. A late thirteenth-century treatise, *De oculo morali*, attributed to Peter of Limoges, provides us with an example of the interest in physics combined with allegory.[32] Peter deals with refracted and unrefracted light and, in agreement with the most authoritative writers of his time, holds that unrefracted rays are superior to refracted ones. From this he draws the conclusion that unrefracted ('morally best') rays are better propagators of reality than refracted light rays. Vision in this life, says

29 On Grosseteste and the *lux/lumen* distinction, see L. E. Lynch, 'The Doctrine of Divine Ideas and Illumination in Robert Grosseteste, Bishop of Lincoln', *Mediaeval Studies* 3 (1941) 161–73; Lindberg, *Theories of Vision*, pp. 94–103; see also Miller, 'Three Mirrors', p. 271.

30 On Roger Bacon, see L. Thorndike, 'Roger Bacon and Experimental Method in the Middle Ages', *Philosophical Review* 23 (1914) 271–98; G. Federici Vescovini, 'Ruggero Bacone e la "Perspectiva" come scienza sperimentale', in *Studi sulla prospettiva medievale*, Pubblicazioni della Facolta' di Lettere e Filosofia 16 (Turin, 1965), 1–286, pp. 53–76; Lindberg, *Theories of Vision*, pp. 107–16. On John Pecham, see D. C. Lindberg, 'The *Perspectiva communis* of John Pecham: Its Influence, Sources, and Content', *Archives internationales d'histoire des sciences* 18 (1965) 37–53. On the influence of Bacon, Pecham, and Witelo, see D. C. Lindberg, 'Lines of Influence in Thirteenth-Century Optics: Bacon, Witelo, and Pecham', *Speculum* 46 (1971) 66–83.

31 The interest in optics at the papal curia in the late 13th century is mentioned by Lindberg in his *Theories of Vision*, pp. 117, 255.

32 The example of the *De oculo morali* is discussed in D. L. Clark, 'Optics for Preachers: the *De oculo morali* by Peter of Limoges', *Michigan Academician* 9 (1977) 329–43, on which my analysis is based.

Peter, occurs only by means of refracted, and therefore weak, light, whereas in the glory of the final resurrection man will be able to see by means of straight lines. We retrace our steps along a 'scientific' path to the obscurity of this world's vision referred to by Paul.

Even before Peter of Limoges, Roger Bacon had argued something similar in his *Opus Maius*; in this he held that sinners reflect and hold God's grace off from them, while in the good, God's grace is comparable to the light that falls perpendicularly and is unrefracted.[33] According to Peter there is a physiological reason for saying that the good have a 'mirror' that receives divine light. The mirror that makes for improvement in the imperfect vision of this world is the internal sense, which is situated in the frontal area of the brain where, in binocular vision, the rays from the eyes meet. The theory of visual rays accepted by Bacon and Pecham – with the subordinate role attributed to them of transforming sensory stimuli into perception – is also accepted by Peter of Limoges, who interprets it in a moral context: Peter endows lascivious women with the ability to emit poisonous rays, which all righteous men should steer clear of. The circulation of a moral treatise giving contemporary scholars' views of traditional and modern theories of optics in language suitable for the non-specialist reader shows once again that science itself was among the influences that led to wide acceptance of the mirror metaphor.

The thirteenth century, the period of greatest interest in problems associated with optics, also witnesses the appearance of the allegorical work that most strongly influenced English medieval literature – the *Roman de la Rose*. The *Roman* is vital for our analysis, since the meanings the mirror metaphor assumes in it are both diverse and significant. It is important to point out here that Guillaume de Lorris reworks the myth of Narcissus in the context of courtly love in the first part, while in the second Jean de Meun gives Nature a long digression on optics, mirrors, and dreams. When Jean first set himself to complete his predecessor's work he called it *Le Mirouer aus Amoureus* (*The Mirror for Lovers*; 10651) in virtue of the positive effect the book might be expected to have on lovers.[34] In spite of various 'modern' interpretations of Guil-

33 *The 'Opus Maius' of Roger Bacon*, trans. R. B. Burke (Philadelphia, 1928), pt. IV, pp. 238–9.

34 On the myth of Narcissus in the *Roman*, see T. D. Hill, 'Narcissus, Pygmalion, and the Castration of Saturn: Two Mythographical Themes in the *Roman de la Rose*',

laume's use of the Narcissus myth – interpretations which tend to see Narcissus as man divided between self and the image of self[35] – the adaptation to medieval canons in the episode of the love of 'Echo, une haute dame' (a great lady; 1444), a love which Narcissus spurns, is evident: the story serves as a warning to court ladies not to resist love. Narcissus died because of the folly he committed by falling in love with his own shadow (1492 ff). From the fountain in the myth we move on to the fountain in the garden: at first the lover is frightened by this fountain because of its associations with Narcissus, but then, by means of two wonderful crystals, the fountain displays all its power to reflect the most minute details – with no falsification. Without underestimating the theses put forward by C. S. Lewis, who compares the power of the crystals to the magic of eyes and mirrors, and by J. Frappier, who sees the Neoplatonic conception of *speculum mundi* in the garden's power to reflect,[36] we can see that the mirror which reflects objects without modifying them is seen here as positive. In the second part of the *Roman* Jean takes up the theme of the fountains of Narcissus, but now it is seen as sinister and dangerous – and above all untruthful, since it can reflect only half of the surrounding garden, by contrast with the fountain of life.

To Guillaume's courtly, aesthetic view Jean opposes a more realistic and scientific conception of reality. The title Jean gives the *Roman* – *Le Mirouer aus Amoureus* – means both mirror *for* and mirror *of* lovers; it thus has the double function of giving a normative picture of the art of love, and of reflecting lovers just as they are.[37] Later on Nature expounds

Studies in Philology 71 (1974) 404–26; D. F. Hult, 'The Allegorical Fountain: Narcissus in the *Roman de la Rose*', *Romanic Review* 72 (1981) 125–48, and by the same author, *Self-fulfilling Prophecies, Readership and Authority in the First Roman de la Rose* (Cambridge, 1986), ch. 4.

All quotations of the *Roman* are from E. Langlois, ed., *Le Roman de la Rose par Guillaume de Lorris et Jean de Meun* (Paris, 1914–24), 5 vols; English translation by C. Dahlberg, *The Romance of the Rose* (Hanover and London, 1986).

35 Frappier, 'Variations sur le thème du miroir', pp. 149–52, and especially E. Köhler, 'Narcisse, la fontaine d'Amour et Guillaume de Lorris', *Journal des Savants* (Avril–Juin 1963) 86–103, pp. 93ff., tend to see the fountain in a positive way as a means of regeneration. A. M. F. Gunn, *The Mirror of Love. A Reinterpretation of 'The Romance of the Rose'* (Lubbock, Texas, 1952), interprets the two parts as a whole, so that the two images of Narcissus are seen as complementary. This is also the thesis of Robertson, *A Preface to Chaucer*, pp. 91–8, and of J. V. Fleming, *The Roman de la Rose: A Study in Allegory and Iconography* (Princeton, 1969), pp. 92–103.

36 Cf. C. S. Lewis, *The Allegory of Love* (Oxford, 1936), pp. 128–9, and Frappier, 'Variations sur le thème du miroir', p. 151, respectively.

37 The distinction is found in P. J. Eberle, 'The Lovers' Glass: Nature's Discourse on Optics and the Optical Design of the *Romance of the Rose*', *University of Toronto*

at length on the various types of mirrors, lenses and prisms. These reflecting surfaces have magnifying and reducing power, they can create the colours of the rainbow, and they can give both true and false images of the world. Mirrors are then seen in all their possible applications from microscopes to telescopes, from 'burning glasses' to magic distorting mirrors. As Eberle has pointed out, the properties attributed to mirrors resemble, and deliberately imitate, the rules of rhetoric, such as *abbreviatio*, *amplificatio* and the use of *colores*.[38]

By choosing Nature as the exponent of a long theoretical disquisition on mirrors Jean, unlike Guillaume, intends to offer a series of possible perspectives on nature's works and their reflection in the *Roman* both on a metaphorical level and in its content. By contrast with the single perspective of courtly tradition employed by Guillaume, with its abstractions conforming to the conventions of personification allegory, Jean offers a system of knowledge that is not necessarily at odds with his predecessor's tradition but which integrates it into his own world-view with its multiple approaches to various questions. Jean's quotations from Euclid and Aristotle as sources from the past, and Alhazen ('Regarz' – 18043) as the greatest Arab authority available in translation, show him to be profoundly interested in the findings of this new science. The crystals in the fountain which in the first part faithfully reflect the *hortus conclusus* are able, in Jean's version, to reflect only half of the garden around it: and similarly the world of chivalry, in whose rules Guillaume seems to believe blindly, is no more than a part of reality and does not comprehend the whole of it. To the variety of earthly mirrors is opposed the mirror of divine Providence: *miroer pardurable* (eternal mirror; 17468), *bel miroer poli* (beautiful polished mirror; 17473). Providence is 'Cil miroers c'est il meïsmes, / De cui commencement preïsmes' (This mirror is the same one from which we took our beginning; 17471–2).

Even though Jean does not quote Grosseteste directly, he is strongly influenced by his theories, especially in his description of the moon as optical glass and in his treatment of the influences exerted by celestial bodies.[39] Even the eye can be considered an optical glass subject to

Quarterly 46 (1977) 241–62 (to which I am much indebted), and then discussed in K. Brownlee, 'Reflections in the *Miroër aus Amoreus*. The Inscribed Reader in Jean de Meun's *Roman de la Rose*', in J. D. Lyons and S. G. Nichols, eds., *Mimesis. From Mirror to Method, Augustine to Descartes* (Hanover and London, 1982), pp. 60–70, p. 60.

38 Eberle, 'The Lovers' Glass', pp. 244ff.

39 *Ibidem*, pp. 248–55.

optical illusions, such as Nature supposes will occur on the basis of the physiology then current. The detailed account of the various optical illusions human nature is subject to because of dreams and strong emotions is relevant in a dream-vision poem born of passionate love. Jean's *Mirouer* has the manifest aim of lifting the veil of allegory and rendering explicit the elements that characterize the dream-vision: 'Puis voudra si la chose espondre / Que riens ne s'i pourra repondre' (Then he will want to explicate the affair in such a way that nothing can remain hidden; 10603–4). Quite deliberately he follows the part concerning mirrors with the treatise on dreams and illusions: equally deliberately the title indicates a mirror of and for lovers. By describing the physical disorders that amorous passion can give rise to in terms of optics, Nature clarifies by means of science Guillaume's allegorical obscurities, and she also provides an explanation of the two shining stones that lie at the bottom of the fountain. The various characters contained in the optical glass are then none other than facets of the Amant, and by embodying his various features they make them manifest. We find here a further motive for Jean's title. An ideal Amant, such as Guillaume assumes can exist, is negated by the irreducible complexity of the influence of love: similarly on earth it is impossible that there should exist one mirror only, since the perfect mirror is God. There are many mirrors, and also one mirror which, however, can never reproduce faithfully the source of what it reflects. All mirrors, even the most complex ones, distort: Guillaume's stones do not reflect the whole garden but only half of it. Once the hypothesis of the reduction of the whole to a part is accepted, it can be seen that the consequence is fragmented vision. Thus the final unveiling with the taking of the Rose is explained, in that it is shown for what it actually is. But even this is an illusory, transient vision, like everything that forms part of the world. Everything must be studied in the smallest detail, however with the aim of understanding its true nature – which is human, and therefore imperfect. The justification for considering the *Roman* a single whole, a problem which has engaged the attention of many critics, is contained in the multiplicity of nature itself, and because of this, the dichotomy Guillaume/Jean becomes an erroneous formulation of the problem. Jean does not oppose Guillaume's idealism; on the contrary, by accepting it, he defines its limits.

The mirror is present both as a material object for study and as a metaphor. The *Roman* takes over and synthesizes the vast tradition of research into mirrors and the effects they produce: the treatment this tradition is given is proof of the high status the subject had been accorded by that time. It seems also to have been intended as an encyclopedic mirror of knowledge. The theme of love, as Jean handles it, is all-embracing, both because its effects are many and various, and because by its very nature it is changeable. The long discussion on dreams and illusions, with the list of the various types of vision, is an indication of the metalinguistic labour Jean carries out in order to evaluate the structure of a poetic work in general, and of his own in particular. In art as in Nature, illusion and multiplicity dominate: a single answer does not exist. Jean's art, his poetry, aims at providing all possible answers to questions concerning love. Moreover, the poem as a mirror for lovers also incorporates the reader's particular experience and compares it with other experiences: in this way it acts as a corrective mirror.

As Brownlee has convincingly pointed out,[40] Jean addresses four social categories, from 'ideal lovers' to clerics, and the authorial stand, based on reason and experience, is quite clear:

> Onc riens n'en dis, mien escient,
> Coment qu'il m'aut contrariant,
> Qui ne seit en escrit trouvé
> E par esperiment prouvé,
> Ou par raison au meins prouvable,
> A cui qu'el seit desagreable.
>
> (Nevertheless, in my opinion, no matter who disputes it, I have never said anything that may not be found in writing, either proved by experience or at least capable of being proved by reason, no matter whom it may displease; 15293–8.)

Jean's authority is firmly based on the writings of the *auctores* of the past, and on the new experimental science; and it is in any case founded on reason, whether it is acceptable or not.

From this brief analysis of the *Roman* emerge the remarkable richness of the mirror metaphor and the didactic function of the metaphor itself. Various traditions converge and form that web of mirrorings that make up the *Roman* and thus justify the title given to it by Jean. By means of this metaphor the poet tries to suggest that, just as Nature generates by a

40 Brownlee, *Reflections in the Miroër aus Amoreus*, pp. 65ff. On the philosophical ideas behind the *Roman*, see K. L. Lynch, *The High Medieval Dream Vision. Poetry, Philosophy, and Literary Form* (Stanford, 1988), ch. 4.

series of correspondences, so art generates by mimesis images that are true to reality in all its variety.

We must not forget the use of the metaphor in mystical literature, where the Pauline distinction between the obscurity of human knowledge and communion with God in Paradise underlies the mystical experience itself.[41] By virtue of the likeness between creature and Creator, the mystic can aspire to ascend towards the supreme knowledge which is the contemplation of God. When mystics deal with the spiritual progress of the soul towards God, they associate the ladder metaphor with that of the mirror: the ladder is the means by which the distance between the two poles, human and supernatural, is bridged – as Richard of St Victor explains:

> Ubi ad alta quidem ascendere volumus, scala quidem uti solemus, nos qui homines sumus et volare non possumus. Rerum ergo visibilium similitudine pro scala utamur, ut quae in semetipsis per speciem videre non valemus, ex ejusmodi specula et velut per speculum videre mereamur.
>
> (When we wish to ascend, we naturally use a ladder, we who are men and unable to fly. Then let us use as a ladder the similitude of visible things, so that the things we cannot see by direct vision we may become able to see from this watch-tower and as though in a mirror; *De Trinitate* V, vi.)[42]

Richard points out the limit of the range of human vision, and explains how this limit can be overcome with the help of a ladder: if a man climbs up closer to God on the ladder, his sight is enabled to reflect, as if in a mirror, God's image. To reach the highest stage of vision, which is contemplation, a long, gradual process of speculative reasoning is required. The mirror metaphor serves the mystics as a means by which to approach God, but it is Christ who bridges the gap between God's omnipotence and man's finite nature. Christ Incarnate made possible the relationship between human and spiritual, finite and infinite. The complex mystical experience is compared by some critics to the mirror stage of which Jacques Lacan speaks.[43] According to his theory, the six-

41 On the use of the metaphor by the mystics, see Louth, *Origins*, pp. 79ff., and Bradley, 'The Speculum Image', passim.

42 Quoted in Goldin, *The Mirror of Narcissus*, p. 8.

43 For a psychoanalytical (Lacanian) interpretation of the mirror image among female mystics, see S. Beckwith, 'A Very Material Mysticism: The Medieval Mysticism of

to eighteen-months-old child is in a mirror phase, during which he grasps the idea of a complete self by identifying it with the image he sees in the mirror. But this identification also leads to the discovery of difference, to the desire for unity with the image in the mirror. In this way the child compares himself with the other, which is represented by his mother, by other children, and by spatial-temporal limitations.[44] If, as Wilden says, the mirror phase is a 'vision of harmony by a being in discord',[45] then we realize that this definition can fit mystical experience: here the soul is distant from its Creator, but it aspires to oneness with Him through Christ. By his earthly presence Christ exalts and justifies the social and family roles, to the extent of giving absolute authority to social norms, especially family ties, of fundamental importance in consolidating the power of the emerging middle class.

The enormously wide circulation of the mirror metaphor in the Middle Ages is due then to a series of impulses which can be summed up in the desire and the search for analogy within a conceptual system dominated by correspondence. The final outcome of the metaphor is moral teaching, or at least an indication of how the soul's progress towards God can be assisted. The principle of *imitatio* is central in the Middle Ages: every work of art is a re-creation of what already exists.[46] The mirror as a surface that reflects the objects placed in front of it is the perfect vehicle for a 'mimetic' conception of art and its ethical justification. As Alastair Fowler maintains, the important thing is not how many works are entitled *speculum*, since in the Middle Ages, given the depersonalization of the frequently anonymous poet, the title is not an essential element;[47] food for thought instead is the common didactic basis of works that make wide use of the mirror metaphor. Allegory is the means that the medieval author employs to treat the fundamental human themes: death, salvation, love, man's view of the world. The mirror as a metaphor within the allegorical text makes it possible to place the individual

Margery Kempe', in D. Aers, ed., *Medieval Literature: Criticism, Ideology & History* (Brighton, 1986), pp. 34–57, especially pp. 41–8.

44 See J. Lacan, 'Le stade du miroir comme formateur de la fonction du "je" ', in *Écrits I* (Paris, 1966), pp. 89–97.

45 A. Wilden, *Speech and Language in Psychoanalysis: Jacques Lacan* (Baltimore and London, 1981), p. 174.

46 See C. S. Lewis, *The Discarded Image* (Cambridge, 1964), ch. VIII. On the 'difference' of medieval culture, see S. Medcalf, 'On reading books from a half-alien culture', in S. Medcalf, ed., *The Later Middle Ages* (London, 1981), pp. 1–55.

47 Fowler, 'Through the Looking-glass', p. 872.

man and the particular sin within the universal ambit and context; it also serves as a vehicle for a comparison with the ideal. On one hand the receptive capacity of the mirror gives a representation of reality as it is; on the other, the relationship established with the universal, whether this be God (in the mirror of God) or beauty (in the courtly mirror), implies that a process leading towards moral improvement has been set in train in the Christian conviction that life is a pilgrimage, a quest leading towards union with God in the afterlife.

The double value of the mirror is illustrated in the first half of the fifteenth century by the Flemish painter Jan van Eyck in his picture on *The Arnolfini Wedding*. The most authoritative interpretation of the painting, Panofsky's, gives us a double reading, symbolic and realistic, whereby the nuptial chamber is at one and the same time a real place and a *thalamus Virginis*.[48] The picture can also be read typologically, and the presence of the mirror with its reflected image authorizes such a reading.[49]

The bride and groom are represented realistically in a real room decorated in typical fifteenth-century style; an ascending line runs from the dog, passes through the mirror, and ends at the candelabra. The position of the figures recalls many paintings of the Fall of Man, with Adam and Eve separated by the tree of the forbidden fruit.[50] This tree, which appears as the wood of the mirror-frame, is here replaced by ten scenes from the passion and resurrection of Christ, and these refer to the transformation of the Fall into the Redemption through Christ's Incarnation. The iconographic arrangement associates the couple with the topos of the Fall, while the mirror-frame – which is made up of ten mirrors – places the young man and woman within the redeeming action of Christ. But the series of references does not end here. The action being carried out within the limits of the painting has a witness, the painter, who – like the viewer – forms part of the wider world than can be glimpsed in the subsidiary details reflected by the convex mirror. This mirror functions not only metaphorically, by connecting the act of observation to the wedding, and to the history of the world that is always

48 E. Panofsky, *Early Netherlandish Painting: Its Origins and Character* (Cambridge, Mass., 1964), pp. 202–3. His view is accepted by H. Schwarz, 'The Mirror in Art', *The Art Quarterly* 15 (1952) 97–118, pp. 97–9.

49 I am very much indebted to Wall's typological interpretation of the painting: J. N. Wall, Jr., 'Jan van Eyck's Art of Persuasion: The *Arnolfini Wedding Portrait* as Christian Proclamation', in A. L. Deneef and M. T. Hester, eds., *Renaissance Papers 1981* (Durham, North Carolina, 1982), pp. 71–86.

50 *Ibidem*, pp. 74–6.

present to God, but also functions as an optical glass, which widens the bounds of the painting by offering further information, such as the door and two figures peeping round it. The act the painter witnesses, and in which he is included by means of the circular form of the mirror-frame which contains it, serves to point up the circular nature of human experience in its relationship to God. In the sacrament of marriage the Arnolfinis partake of the saving power of God in Christ, and like them the viewer is called on to act for his own salvation. The painting, which is composed with a view to including as much as possible of the surrounding world, excludes the viewer precisely because of the limits imposed by selection – thus reminding him of the 'otherness' of the scene. A pictorial work has nonetheless the same analogical power as a literary work: just as the ten scenes from the life of Christ transform the image of the Fall into one of Redemption, so van Eyck's attempt to use the convex mirror to enlarge the vision of the world around the newly-married couple causes the viewer to feel himself involved in a similar process of transformation.

According to Wall, the mirror therefore has the function of projecting the events *in* the painting (the relationship between the resurrection of Christ and the Arnolfinis' wedding) *out* into the world of the viewer (the relationship between painter and observer),[51] so as to suggest a close analogical relationship between the particular event (the wedding) which is already set within the universal in the painting, and the particular event which is the perception by the observer, who is led to act in accordance with the message from God for which the artist has served as intermediary. By means of the mechanism of image-likeness *inside* and *outside* the painting, the observer succeeds in recognizing himself as a related part of the harmony between natural and spiritual.

From all the examples examined there emerges the paradox that lies at the origin of what may be termed specularity: it lends itself to exploitation in a cosmological conception, Platonic in origin, which attempts to reconcile – while at the same time recognizing their reciprocal difference – the transient and the eternal, the natural and the supernatural. If, on the one hand, the image reflected in the mirror – being momentary – lacks historicity, on the other it is precisely thanks to its resistance to codification that it can become a receptacle for ineffable, mysterious, elusive contents. The reflected image becomes pregnant with signifi-

51 Wall, 'Jan van Eyck's Art of Persuasion', pp. 79–80.

cance, both of things ephemeral and things eternal, precisely because it is a-temporal. For there to be a reflected image, there must be a model of which the reflected image is an exact copy. The mirror's function, therefore, is to put the copy into relation with the model or first image. One of the values of specularity is impermanence, so that whoever, like Narcissus or the fool, believes that his own reflected image is eternal mistakes the copy for the model – and dies of his mistake. The other meaning is that which, by means of the 'recollection' of the model, by likeness, leads the particular back to the universal, whose traces the copy contains: in the final analysis this means that man is led back to God, since he is made in God's image and likeness.

The power of the specular process to indicate the one and the whole, the microcosm and the macrocosm, gives rise to the widespread use of the metaphor in literature; and it is this versatility that makes possible the grouping of the various texts according to the meaning given to the metaphor. Classifications are, however, very difficult to draw up and are to a certain extent arbitrary, especially when they are applied to a metaphor like that of the mirror, which stands not just for something else but for its opposite as well.[52] God is a mirror in which we can see our imperfections; man is a mirror (even a single individual man, such as the sovereign or the poet); the Bible is the mirror of the word of God. The adaptability of the metaphor is evident: God as mirror is the model; the sovereign as mirror may be a model of perfection, but also of imperfection, according to the parable of John Chrysostom that I have quoted above.[53]

The literary forms that contain the metaphor are various. In addition to the corrective mirror there is the encyclopedic mirror, very much in use because it condensed the vast reality of the world: and there were also handbooks. As the example of *The Arnolfini Wedding* testifies, mirrors were convex and remained so until the seventeenth century, thus allowing reflection and reduction. The printed book, which makes its appearance in the second half of the fifteenth century – and in which pre-existing material is re-presented in condensed form – is declared to have the same function as the mirror. It is no chance happening that the works William Caxton printed include the *Mirror of the World*. Man appears more and more frequently as a metaphorical mirror: if Troilus is a mirror of 'goodlyheede', this is because he personifies the idea of the

52 For a comprehensive classification of mirror types, see Grabes, *The Mutable Glass*.
53 See p. 5.

beautiful; if Cicero is a mirror of eloquence, this is because he embodies the idea of eloquence. Behind all these definitions there lies the resemblance between reflection (copy) and original (model). When applied to the sovereign the metaphor is found much more widely, since the sovereign can embody public and private virtues, or else be a negative example as a personification of the worst vices. He should indeed be a positive model in which his subjects can be reflected, and not a negative *exemplum* of vices (which a sovereign must shun, and against which his subjects must rebel). The Middle Ages see a fine flowering of *Specula principum* and *De regimine principum*[54] which, taking the pseudo-Aristotelian *Secretum* as their model, instruct the sovereign on right behaviour by means of the exemplary figures of virtues and vices created by the poet. This is perhaps one of the most productive lines of development in the whole of medieval literature, both because it was perfectly adapted to the didactic function of a work addressed to a man responsible for his country's destiny, and because it allowed the poet to play a progressively more important role as court advisor – to the extent of becoming a public official at his sovereign's side. In the various *De Casibus* and *Fall of Princes*, the mirror metaphor serves as a warning. By drawing a comparison between himself and men of the past, and by framing his own individual experience within what is universal, the sovereign can observe the inevitability of change not only for the common man, but for everyone – and he must accept these observations and act accordingly. Here the metaphor is connected with the topoi of the wheel of Fortune, *contemptus mundi* and *memento mori*, in order that the reversals of fortune and the inevitability of death should always be present in the minds of the powerful.[55] History is thus a mirror of the past – with positive and negative value – which contains examples either to follow or to avoid.

A woman – usually a noblewoman – may also be a mirror of virtues associated with her high rank: purity and almost divine beauty. When the poet presents his lady as a mirror, he acknowledges her superior beauty and stresses the remoteness that her social status involves. In poetry the didactic rather than the epistemological function of the metaphor is emphasized, even if knowledge serves as the basis for moral

54 See, as an example, T. Hoccleve's *Regement of Princes*, which is discussed later in the book.

55 The most important study of topoi is still Curtius, *European Literature and the Latin Middle Ages*. On the role of Fortune in medieval literature, see H. R. Patch, *The Goddess Fortuna in Mediaeval Literature* (Cambridge, Mass., 1927).

improvement. In this case, what is important is the qualitative difference between the exemplary figure (the lady) and the observer, because it is precisely his realization of this distance that leads the poet to recognize his own inferiority and to begin his progress towards an eventual change of heart.[56] The mirror of virtue is not always the beloved's face but often only a part of it: her eye is capable of mediating as a reflecting surface between the source – that is, the ideal – and the lover to whom the reflection is directed. The image of the lady's eye as a means of mediation between the poet and the transcendental is frequently used by Dante and the Dolce Stil Novo poets. In *Paradiso* XXVIII, 4–9, Beatrice's eyes enable the pilgrim to see a reflection of divine light,[57] thus carrying out their function of transmitting knowledge of a celestial world to mortal intellect. Beatrice's role is even higher, since the image reflected in her eyes is identical with the light from the angelic circles; now that Dante, like Beatrice, is ready to receive direct illumination from God, he is able to recognize the nature of this image. The pilgrim has ventured beyond the mirror of the created world and is enabled to stand before God's mirror. Just as the pilgrim ascends towards his final goal through different stages of knowledge, so the poet adapts

56 The role played by the eyes in courtly love is discussed in G. Favati, 'Una traccia di cultura neoplatonica in Chrétien de Troyes: il tema degli occhi come specchio', in *Studi in onore di Carlo Pellegrini*, Biblioteca di Studi Francesi 2 (1963) 3–13; R. H. Cline, 'Heart and Eyes', *Romance Philology* 25 (1972) 263–97; L. K. Donaldson-Evans, 'Love's Fatal Glance: Eye Imagery and Maurice Scève's Délie', *Neophilologus* 62 (1978) 202–11.

57 come in lo specchio fiamma di doppiero
vede colui che se n'alluma retro,
prima che l'abbia in vista o in pensiero,
e sé rivolge per veder se 'l vetro
li dice il vero, e vede ch'el s'accorda
con esso come nota con suo metro.

(as one who sees in a mirror the flame of a torch
which is lighted behind him
before he has it in sight or in thought,
and turns round to see if the glass
tells him the truth, and sees that it accords
with it as a song with its measure; *Par.* XXVIII, 4–9.)

The translation is by C. S. Singleton (Princeton, 1970–75), of the text established by Petrocchi. On the mirror images in *Paradiso*, see the interesting analysis by Miller, 'Three Mirrors', pp. 273–8. On repetition as a mirroring device in the language of *Paradiso*, see J. M. Ferrante, 'Words and Images in the *Paradiso*: Reflections of the Divine', in A. S. Bernardo and A. L. Pellegrini, eds., *Dante, Petrarch, Boccaccio: Studies in the Italian Trecento In Honor of Charles S. Singleton* (Binghamton, New York, 1983), pp. 115–32.

his images, his metaphors, to this new experience. The poem therefore becomes a *speculum* in which the various images form a criss-cross pattern of reflections similar to the play of reflections from the divine light. Just as the Bible is the mirror of the various levels of Creation, so the specular structure of Dante's book mirrors the structure of the cosmos as the divine light is reflected by different mirrors.

This brief reference to Dante provides us with another example of analogy based on the identity of different things: from the eye as an instrument of human knowledge, we arrive at the eye as capable of reflecting divine light.[58] As Beatrice points out disdainfully, the gulf between human experience and divine revelation is immense; but it is precisely thanks to this difference, together with the refinement of the instruments of knowledge, Beatrice's help and God's grace, that Dante succeeds – uncertainly at first but then more confidently – in knowing God. And this gulf between the ideal and objective reality is bridged by the allusive and symbolic language in which a unique experience without equal can be 'told' in a poem. If the highest stage of knowledge is contemplation – by way of speculative reasoning (and the *specula* in the cantos are many) – Dante has given the highest example of knowing in his poem.

To go back now to the eye as mirror, the importance of the metaphor derives from the function of this sense organ in perceiving reality. To achieve knowledge the eye must perceive correctly; seeing correctly – according to the theory of perception in Augustine's *De Trinitate* – allows the soul to orient itself and so form the inner image. Still more important is the distinction between sense image and inner image of the soul, between the image in the eye's mirror and the image in the heart.[59] In Matthew the eye is considered as the light of the body, the window by which the body opens itself to the external world:

> Lucerna corporis tui est oculus tuus. Si oculus tuus fuerit simplex: totum corpus tuum lucidum erit. Si autem oculus tuus fuerit nequam: totum corpus tuum tenebrosum erit. Si ergo lumen, quod in te est, tenebrae sunt: ipsae tenebrae quantae erunt?)

[58] See the optical experiment Beatrice carries out in *Paradiso* II, 94–105, discussed by Miller, 'Three Mirrors', pp. 263–6.

[59] The eye as a mirror is important in Augustine's *De Trinitate* XI, where perception is explained by using sight as an example. Cf. Grabes, *The Mutable Glass*, pp. 83–5.

> (The light of thy body is thy eye. If thy eye be single, thy whole body shall be lightsome. But if thy eye be evil thy whole body shall be darksome. If then the light that is in thee, be darkness: the darkness itself how great shall it be! Matt. 6: 22–3)

The light and lamp metaphor accounts for two elements we have already come across in the eye-soul relationship: the eye must function as a clear mirror capable of perceiving sensitively without obscuring the light that is in the soul by God's will, and of allowing the soul to form the inner, true, image.[60]

To conclude this necessarily limited analysis of the forms of the mirror metaphor, I should like to introduce another analogy – between the mirror and the medieval text. We must remember that, in spite of the invention of printing, literary works were entrusted to scribes for copying until the end of the fifteenth century. This gave the text an 'open' quality by comparison with its printed form, which is definitive unless modified at considerable expense and after the first edition has been available to readers. The manuscript is open to modification within a tradition which envisages art not as a creation, but as a reworking of pre-existing material. For the medieval author, writing meant revealing a little of the particular truth that lies hidden in the system of the letters of the alphabet. Writing is in a certain sense hermeneutics, since it creates a series of texts that allow access and partial decodification of the total system. Writing means imitating, and imitating means elaborating what has already been written. An aspect of this is seen in the widespread practice of glossing, of providing a comment between the lines, hence the close relationship between *auctor* and copyist if – as often happens – they are not one and the same person. As Bruns rightly affirms, '. . . in a manuscript culture the text is not reducible to the letter; that is, a text always contains more than what it says, or what its letters contain, which is why we are privileged to read between the lines, and not to read between them only but to write between them as well, because the text is simply not complete – not fully what it could be, as in the case of the dark story that requires an illuminating retell-

60 On the various meanings of the metaphor of the eye, see W. Deonna, *Le Symbolisme de l'Oeil* (Paris, 1965), pp. 290–300, and the impressive study by G. Schleusener-Eichholz, *Das Auge im Mittelalter*, Bd. I, II (München, 1985).

ing' .[61] The colours of rhetoric help the poet to decorate the *text*, thereby contributing to this operation of disclosure of the hidden meaning – which however will always remain somewhat obscure, open to other future operations of the same kind.

If we compare this way of conceiving writing – with its underlying assumption that a work of art can be reproduced – to the relational function of the mirror as an instrument of knowledge, we will perhaps be better able to understand the reasons for the extensive circulation of the metaphor. Just as the mirror makes possible an 'intertextual' relationship by associating the particular experience with the ideal image by means of the analogy between image-model and image-copy, so the text re-created by the poet from pre-existing texts is the fruit of an imitation which consists in trying to grasp the authority (the ideal) concealed there. Thus originality means something different in medieval culture: if you are original you transcend the text, you are intertextual, in that you read between the lines of the text to find those hidden clues which give the poet the idea of adding his own *inventio* to the material already in existence. The medieval poet's approach to his *mater* is essentially typological, if by typology we mean not only the particular relational analogy between the Old and New Testaments, but also the relationship between pre-existing writings and those of the poet. Both relationships are analogical and interconnected. Is not enlarging on, and reading between the lines of a text an attempt to acquire knowledge which ultimately represents one of the steps by which to reach knowledge of God – whose word is concealed between the lines of Holy Writ?

This way of writing poetry, of re-creating the text by one's own *inventio*, is similar to the functioning of the mirror metaphor. If *inventio* is the part of rhetoric that has to do with the search for and the finding of ideas appropriate to the subject matter – ideas that exist as *copia rerum* in the unconscious and subconscious and which are brought to light by memory – it is clear that this process is analogous to the cognitive process by way of the mirror.

Narrative becomes the *locus* in which the analogy between the rela-

61 G. L. Bruns, 'The Originality of Texts in a Manuscript Culture', *Comparative Literature* 32 (1980) 113–29, p. 125. My indebtedness here is to Bruns' analysis on the openness of medieval texts and to T. M. Greene, *The Light in Troy. Imitation and Discovery in Renaissance Poetry* (New Haven and London, 1982), for the clear distinction between medieval and Renaissance intertextuality (the medieval writer working 'within a system of texts that are all equally available for extension, completion, higher realization', p. 86).

tionship of the two constituent parts and the relationship of the parts in another system is established. Every classic Christian allegory (*Psychomachia, Everyman*, etc.) offers an analogy between the narrative structure and a transcendental, moral structure, that is, what to do to be saved. This analogy is also made possible by the confidence the author places in his reader's ability to extrapolate universal truths from the facts narrated, be it in a context of religious allegory (*Psychomachia*) or of social or psychological allegory (*Roman de la Rose*).

The fourteenth century is also the century of Ockham, who is instrumental in partly undermining the foundations of analogical thought by holding that the universal and the real are two separate things. The universal is not a real thing: it has no objective existence outside the mind, and no psychological existence in the mind.[62] This is not the place for a detailed treatment of Ockham's thought, which I will come back to in the course of my examination of individual texts. However, mention must be made of the fact that Ockham, and the line of philosophical thought he gave rise to, indirectly influenced the process of transformation of the allegorical method. In reality, as Peck has rightly observed with regard to Chaucer (although his statements might also be applied to other authors of the late fourteenth and the fifteenth century) the main problem the authors of the period face is the relationship between words, memory and experience, rather than theories of the validity of philosophical demonstration.[63] To come back to the vitality of the mirror metaphor, however, even though the allegorical method as such is often abandoned (and Chaucer is one of the examples of this tendency) and thus one of the reasons for the spread of the metaphor seems to have disappeared, the convention remains. It is simply differently applied. The cognitive principle of *imitatio* does not lose its value, nor does the emphasis on the moral aim of literary production diminish. Chaucer insists on representing the complexity of human nature by pointing out ambiguities of language, but this does not mean that he is not interested in the deeper realities to which language refers: his purpose is rather to show the difficulty inherent in matching mental constructions to experience. Chaucer certainly knows about the debate

62 On Ockham's role, see G. Leff, *William of Ockham: The Metamorphosis of Scholastic Discourse* (Manchester, 1975), and by the same author, *The Dissolution of the Medieval Outlook* (New York, 1976); see also S. Delany, 'Undoing Substantial Connection: The Late Medieval Attack on Analogical Thought', *Mosaic* 5 (1972) 31–52, pp. 46–51.

63 R. A. Peck, 'Chaucer and the Nominalist Questions', *Speculum* 53 (1978) 745–60, p. 760.

between the Occamists and their opponents, but – as *Troilus and Criseyde* shows – Boethius remains the great *auctoritas* of the past from whom he draws inspiration.[64] Chaucer represents the synthesis of a whole series of questions relative to free will and determinism, in that he accepts Boethius' ideas and shows in his works that reality is very complex and by no means easily fitted into a system of mirrorings and correspondences. As *Troilus* fully exemplifies, Chaucer is perfectly aware that God's love is the one truth for man, yet he also highly values earthly love. Faced with the dilemma of the contrast between natural, pagan love and the Christian love of God, Chaucer shows his greatness in the subtle psychological analysis to which he subjects his characters.

It is this renewed interest in the individual that most clearly distinguishes the Renaissance from the Middle Ages and that requires a different use of the mirror metaphor. It is quite certain that the revival of Neoplatonism by Italian humanists such as Marsilio Ficino could not do without the close-knit system of correspondences in the universe, but little by little the observation point changes and moves progressively from high to low. Interest is centred on man and his social relations, and only *after* this is his relationship to God analysed. This shift of interest is the end of the long, gradual process by which the reciprocity of subject and object was undermined. This reciprocity was already being questioned in England in the late fourteenth century.[65] The mirror metaphor does not lose value in consequence: on the contrary, its primary didactic function gains new validity in a context in which the concept of man as an individual acquires more and more importance.

The authors who will be treated at length here belong to a period that begins with the end of the fourteenth century and ends with the beginning of the sixteenth, the period in which the so-called Chaucerians are at work. The fifteenth century constitutes a very significant phase in the development of the metaphor, and this is of interest to us not only because Chaucerian literature is comparable with the 'mirror' of the works of Chaucer whose greatness it in part reflects, but also because the authors of this period endeavour, while remaining within the bounds of tradition, to offer a new image of pre-existing material.

I shall first examine Chaucer's *Troilus and Criseyde*, a work which

64 Cf. A. J. Minnis, *Chaucer and Pagan Antiquity* (Cambridge, 1982), *passim*.
65 See Fowler, 'Through the Looking-glass', p. 872.

functions until Shakespeare's time and after as a paradigm of courtly romance. Secondly, after offering an analysis of John Lydgate and Thomas Hoccleve as the most significant exponents of the English fifteenth century, I shall discuss John Skelton as a transitional poet writing at the turn of the fifteenth century, and will point out the ways in which he uses the mirror metaphor in his search for new forms of literary expression.

Chaucer's use of the metaphor will be found to be both traditional and innovative. Troilus' mind acts as a mirror to reflect Criseyde's beauty according to the canons of courtly love. At the same time the ambiguity with which the mirror is frequently invested allows Chaucer to underscore, from the very beginning, the conflict between the natural and spiritual dimensions of man. Troilus, as we shall see, makes an earthly being – to whom he offers all his love – the object of his contemplation: not until the end, when he realizes his error, does he recognize the finite nature of such a love. To express this tension between human and spiritual, Chaucer makes use of the double meaning of the mirror metaphor, both positive and negative. Troilus' ascent to the eighth sphere is thus the moment when he discovers that God's 'trouthe' is true love beside which Criseyde's love is seen to be a mere copy.

In his poem *The Temple of Glas* John Lydgate uses the term *glas* to indicate the temple of love, and he characterizes the lady according to the active/passive dichotomy of the mirror metaphor. The lady is seen as a mirror of beauty and virtue, but also as an *exemplum* of suffering and grief. The poem is the mirror of a man's desire for a woman, and of the poet's desire to create a new image of the experience of love, with the emphasis placed on the tensions and conflicting divisions not – as Chaucer had analysed them – in the man, but in the woman. The fact that he used the word *glas* – the material of which mirrors were made by the fifteenth century – in the title is an even clearer indication of the interest Lydgate had in this metaphor.

Chaucer's and Lydgate's use of the metaphor reveals a tendency towards the reflexiveness of thought which was very common in the Late Middle Ages and in the Renaissance. Hoccleve's exploitation of the tradition of the *speculum principis* in his *Regement of Princes* has instead the aim of rendering public the misery of his existence. Hoccleve's innovation consists in his having juxtaposed two *specula* in one work: in the Prologue the mirror of his own unhappy life, and then the mirror of exemplary personages for good or ill that Prince Henry must either imitate or shun. The association between the poet's situation and the education of the prince allows Hoccleve to establish a further connection between the role of the intellectual and that of the king. The autobiographical motif of the depression that Hoccleve did actually fall into adds feasibility to a more realistic interpretation of the mirror metaphor applied to his life as a reflection of the way the future king should behave towards his subjects. The didactic message is still present, but the starting-point is a real situation in a real time, which was dominated by the great problems of war with France and the resulting famine.

John Skelton, my last author, is the most emblematic of the change in the analogical method to which the mirror metaphor belongs. The crisis in values caused by corruption at court and the impossibility of explaining this crisis in traditional language will be seen as the reasons behind the almost obsessive need Skelton showed to experiment with new forms of expression. Skelton reverts to the allegorical form both in the *Bowge of Courte* and *Speke Parott*, but only to demonstrate how threadbare it has become. The *Bowge of Courte* exploits all the apparatus inherited from Chaucer and the Chaucerians; it acts as a negative mirror of life at court, which is characterized by self-interest and fear. The characters in this world are allegorical, but – as we will see – all that is really allegorical about them is their names and the qualities they represent. The strict interdependence between language and higher truth no longer exists, and the consequence of this is a confusion of the real with the apparent, of ends with means. Language and what it can be made to mean are the central concerns in *Speke Parott*, where the mirror metaphor is no longer a mere constituent element of the poem but has become the metaphor of the poet himself and his poem. The parrot/poet is enabled to speak with his meaning hidden under the form of enigmas, but the confusion that derives from this can be read and understood by anyone capable of cracking the reading code. God-inspired, Parott only proves incomprehensible because people are not ready to accept his new way of poetizing. The choice of the parrot as protagonist is significant, since he himself, with his ability to imitate sounds and languages, is a mirror. Parott embodies the dichotomy latent in the image of the mirror in that he is a reflection when he imitates the sounds made by other people, and an image when, by means of the fictional reconstruction of a reality in 'decomposition', he tries to make the reader understand his prophetic message.

For Skelton the function of poetry is to show reality in its various and often contradictory facets, and then recompose them; it may compose them differently from before, just as the mirror reflects the image differently. From the metaphor of the mind as mirror in *Troilus and Criseyde* we thus reach with Skelton the wider metaphor of poetry as a mirror capable of comprehending reality as a whole.

CHAPTER ONE

Troilus' *Good Aventure*: Man's *Trouthe* as a Veiled Mirror of God's *Trouthe*

At the beginning of Book I of *Troilus and Criseyde*, after the scene in the temple, the narrator describes Troilus' state of mind. With remarkable psychological finesse, and with the aid of the mirror image, he reviews the various phases of Troilus' particular attitude to love.

> Thus gan he make a mirour of his mynde
> In which he saugh al holly hire figure,
> And that he wel koude in his herte fynde.
> It was to hym a right good aventure
> To love swich oon, and if he dede his cure
> To serven hir, yet myghte he falle in grace,
> Or ellis for oon of hire servantz pace. (I, 365–71)[1]

This stanza is a synthesis in convex mirror form of Troilus and Criseyde's love story, as it is foreshadowed in Troilus' mind, and as it is known by the narrator who is preparing to tell it. Troilus, whom the reader remembers as scornful of love, is now in thrall to Criseyde's beauty, so that this description fits perfectly the upset that has occurred in the young man's situation. Troilus embodies the ideal of the perfect knight, and for him the Neoplatonic language referring to the mind's mirror with its reflection of Criseyde – and to the heart as arbiter of the rightness of love – is appropriate within the context of a typical courtly love story. There are also indications of the courtly code in the repetition – in two consecutive lines – of the root *serv* in the verb *serven* and in the noun *servantz*, and in the noun *grace* (favour) conceded a lover by his beloved. On the

1 All quotations are from L. D. Benson, ed., *The Riverside Chaucer*, 3rd edn. (Boston, 1987; Oxford, 1988).

other hand, the terms Chaucer uses are not 'innocent': they imply the omniscience of the narrator, who is retelling and not inventing the story.[2] The term *aventure*, associated here with the adjective *good*, refers us straight back to the opening stanza of the poem. It is in this stanza that the aim of the narrative – to describe 'how [Troilus'] aventures fellen / Fro wo to wele, and after out of joie' (I, 3–4) – is announced. In the description of Troilus' state of mind there lurks the threat of the polysemic *aventure*, with its various meanings of happening (neutral in tone), knightly quest, and danger.[3] The middle line of the stanza, 'It was to hym a right good aventure' (I, 368) takes on all its possible meanings. It seems to Troilus that Fortune has smiled on him to make him fall in love, but the narrator is aware of the danger of an event that leaves Troilus 'Ful unavysed of his woo comynge' (I, 378). This stanza acts as an anticipation of the coming events that will prove so disastrous for Troilus.

The story of Troilus and Criseyde is based on irreconcilably contradictory values: Troilus is the mythical representation of constancy and faithfulness, and Criseyde embodies the essence of change and unfaithfulness.[4] The poet/narrator has no choice but to keep these two elements that have come down to him unchanged from the *auctores*. Even if the young couple's love is positive and consonant with the 'lawe of kynde' (I, 238), Criseyde *must* betray a Troilus who *must* remain faithful unto

2 On the role of the narrator in Chaucer's works see D. Mehl, *Geoffrey Chaucer: An Introduction to His Narrative Poetry* (Cambridge, 1986), ch. 3. The relevance of the narrator in *Troilus and Criseyde* is discussed by many critics; see, among others, E. T. Donaldson, 'Criseyde and her Narrator', in *Speaking of Chaucer* (London, 1970), pp. 65–83; R. O. Payne, *The Key of Remembrance: A Study of Chaucer's Poetics* (Westport, Conn., 1973), especially pp. 209–16; B. F. Huppé, 'The Unlikely Narrator: The Narrative Strategy of the *Troilus*', in J. P. Hermann and J. J. Burke, Jr., eds., *Signs and Symbols in Chaucer's Poetry* (Alabama, 1981), pp. 179–94; W. Wetherbee, ' "Per te poeta fui, per te cristiano": Dante, Statius, and the Narrator of Chaucer's *Troilus*', in L. Ebin, ed., *Vernacular Poetics in the Middle Ages*, Studies in Medieval Culture XVI (Kalamazoo, Michigan, 1984), pp. 153–76; D. Lawton, *Chaucer's Narrators* (Cambridge, 1985); D. Mehl, 'Chaucer's Narrator: *Troilus and Criseyde* and the *Canterbury Tales*', in P. Boitani and J. Mann, eds., *The Cambridge Chaucer Companion* (Cambridge, 1986), pp. 213–26.

3 'Aventure' has, according to *MED*, s.v. 'aventure', the meanings of 1. (a) *fate, fortune*; 2. (a) *something that happens, an event*; 3. (a) *danger, risk*; 4. (a) *venture, knightly quest*; 5. *a marvelous thing*; 6. *a tale of adventures*. The various meanings are all exploited by Chaucer, as the examples quoted from the *Troilus* in *MED* show.

4 On the story of Criseyde as a traditional example of an unfaithful woman, see G. Mieszkowski, 'The Reputation of Criseyde 1155–1500', *Transactions of the Connecticut Academy of Arts and Sciences* 43 (1971) 71–153. On Troilus as a faithful lover, see W. H. Brown, Jr., 'A Separate Peace: Chaucer and the Troilus of Tradition', *Journal of English and Germanic Philology* 83 (1984) 492–508.

death. It is precisely *his* faithfulness to the story that he has inherited that makes the narrator intersperse the poem with warning signals of the unhappy ending. These signals do not necessarily involve the narrator's addressing himself directly to the reader/listener; they are rather to be found on a second level of reading and in the more characteristically courtly 'patches'.

If we take the above-quoted stanza as a paradigm, we will notice that the opening metaphor of the mirror of the mind – which appears both in the *Romaunt* and in the *Boece* and represents a departure from the *Filostrato* – is ambivalent.[5] Unlike the *Filostrato*, where Troiolo calls to mind Criseida's physical charms, this stanza shows Troilus making of his mind a mirror bearing the impress of Criseyde's whole person. The value of the ambiguity of the mirror metaphor is made clear by analogy with the metaphor in the *Boece*:

> *thilke Stoycienis wenden that the sowle*
> *had ben nakid of itself, as a mirour or a clene*
> *parchemyn, so that alle figures most first*
> *comen fro thinges fro withoute into soules,*
> *and ben emprientid into soules.* (*Boece* V, m. 4, 11–15)

Added to this is the objection that the soul cannot offer 'ymages ydel and / vein in the manere of a mirour' (*Boece* V, m. 4, 26–7).[6] The *figure* that Troilus' mind encloses is something external, something vain and void, to be 'seen' with physical eyes. The obsessive presence of the isotopy of 'seeing'/'looking' in the lovers' meeting in the temple is sublimated here, together with the ambiguous image, in Troilus' mind.

The ambivalence of earthly and supernatural that the mirror image seems to suggest is then dissolved in the everyday atmosphere of the courtly world, to which the commonplace concerning the knight's ser-

5 The metaphor of the mind as a mirror is found in *The Romaunt of the Rose* ('For Thought anoon thanne shall bygynne, / As fer, God wot, as he can fynde, / To make a mirrour of his mynde; / For to biholde he wole not lette.' – 2804–7) and in *Boece* (V, m. 4, 11–13). Whereas Boccaccio's Troiolo praises Criseida's beauty, Chaucer emphasizes Troilus' mental power which is capable of embracing Criseyde's 'figure'. The new edition, *Geoffrey Chaucer: Troilus and Criseyde*, by B. A. Windeatt (London and New York, 1984), is particularly useful for a study of the analogies and differences between *Troilus* and *Filostrato*.

6 A detailed analysis of the metaphor in *Troilus* and of its derivation from the *Consolatio* is found in K. Reichl's essay, 'Chaucer's *Troilus*: Philosophy and Language', in P. Boitani, ed., *The European Tragedy of Troilus* (Oxford, 1989), pp. 133–52.

vice refers. The central mirror metaphor offers the choice of analysing Troilus and Criseyde's love story in terms of a conflict between the natural and the spiritual dimension of man, similar to the conflict Paul outlined in his Epistles to the Corinthians.[7] An interpretation of *Troilus and Criseyde* that may help to lessen the contrast between the story's development and its final conclusion is to be found in the passage from a condition of impossible natural and spiritual oneness on earth to an acceptance of the natural as something *other* than the spiritual, with the final consciousness of the distance that separates the two dimensions. This type of analysis makes it possible to explain and justify the narrator's relationship to Troilus and Criseyde: he sees them as bound by a love that each lives wholeheartedly, but which for Troilus is founded on the fusion of earthly and supernatural and for Criseyde on things of the earth alone. Chaucer is reworking a pagan story with a pagan character, and he tries to maintain 'historical' faithfulness in treating his 'matere';[8] during the development of *his* tale, however, he becomes increasingly aware of the providential vision of history that cannot fail to influence even the pagan world. The ending to Book V is not Christian Chaucer giving the story a Christian turn: it consists rather of his acknowledgement that natural love is not to be confused with God's love. The conversion Paul speaks of is impossible for Troilus, but awareness of the finite nature of man's love in relation to God's grows in him, and with his ascent to the eighth sphere he opens his heart towards an unknown reality. Chaucer's consciousness of the differences in time and language[9] does not prevent him from turning his hand to one more reworking of a subject already amply treated by a long series of *auctores*, or from being the first to combine a large number of different genres in a narrative.[10]

7 On the ambiguity of the mirror metaphor in Paul's Epistles, see Introduction, pp. 3–7.

8 On Chaucer's sense of history in relation to pagan antiquity, see A. J. Minnis, *Chaucer and Pagan Antiquity* (Cambridge, 1982).

9 Cf. the often quoted stanzas at the beginning of Book II (ll. 22–35).

10 For a discussion of the different genres of which Chaucer makes use in the *Troilus*, see P. Boitani, *English Medieval Narrative in the 13th & 14th Centuries* (Cambridge, 1982), ch. 6.2, where all the major themes of *Troilus* are thoroughly examined; and more recently, B. Windeatt, 'Classical and Medieval Elements in Chaucer's *Troilus*', in Boitani, *The European Tragedy of Troilus*, pp. 111–31. Chaucer's indebtedness to Boethius was first analysed in Jefferson's pioneering work: B. L. Jefferson, *Chaucer and the Consolation of Philosophy of Boethius* (Princeton, 1917). On the medieval conception of tragedy, see M. E. McAlpine, *The Genre of Troilus and Criseyde* (Ithaca and London, 1978).

This consciousness also allows us to see the possibility of a connection between the values of the pagan world and those of the Christian world, through the appeal to God at the end and at the beginning of the poem:

> And ek for me preieth to God so dere
> That I have myght to shewe, in som manere,
> Swich peyne and wo as Loves folk endure,
> In Troilus unsely aventure. (I, 32–5)

> Thow oon, and two, and thre, eterne on lyve,
> That regnest ay in thre, and two, and oon,
> Uncircumscript, and al maist circumscrive,
> Us from visible and invisible foon
> Defende, and to thy mercy, everichon,
> So make us, Jesus, for thi mercy, digne,
> For love of mayde and moder thyn benigne.
> Amen. (V, 1863–9)

That the poem is based on a series of parallels, on a kind of 'dissimilar similitude',[11] is clear from the very beginning of Book I, when the narrator prepares to embark upon *his own aventure*, namely to describe Troilus' *aventures*. The narrator declares himself an unworthy servant of love's servants, but hopes, with God's help, to be able to relate 'the double sorwes' (I, 54). There is, then, a clear association between self-depreciation and self-confidence in his ability to organize the available material into a written work – 'Thise woful vers, that wepen as I write' (I, 7). Just as Troilus' mind makes a mirror of itself to enclose the memory of Criseyde, changing it into a reflection of something ideal, so Chaucer's mind becomes a mirror to comprehend the love story and to offer it as the image of something more profound, more complex and more complicated than the historical model suggests. If it is true that time and change, and change in time, are among the basic concerns of the poem,[12] then the narrator may intervene directly to modify the

11 D. W. Rowe, *O Love O Charite! Contraries Harmonized in Chaucer's Troilus* (Carbondale and Edwardsville, 1976) uses Dionysius the Areopagite's *The Divine Names* to define the law of 'dissimilar similitude' which is to be found at the root of Chaucer's idea of the universe in *Troilus and Criseyde* (pp. 60–2, 71–2, 84–5, 99–100). Although I find Rowe's observations about 'contraries' very interesting, I agree with I. Bishop, *Chaucer's Troilus and Criseyde: A Critical Study* (Bristol, 1981), when he states that Rowe's account of 'contraries harmonized' is often unconvincing (p. 111). Bishop's fine reading of the narrative structure of the poem is very useful.

12 Time and change are discussed by J. M. Ganim, 'Consciousness and Time in *Troilus*

'matere' towards a Christian use of such a famous story, just so long as his modifications do not infringe on tradition.

Chaucer chooses to narrate a love story, but he does not because of this forget to block in the state of the war between Greeks and Trojans:[13] he connects the war outside Troy's walls with the 'calkulynge' (I, 71) of Calchas who, with his departure and defection to the Greeks, is guilty of the first of a long line of betrayals. Alongside the traitor Calchas looms Fortune, with her ever-turning wheel.[14] Chaucer makes a great deal of Calchas' wickedness so that it will point up the fear that assails Criseyde, twice abandoned, first when her husband died and then when her father fled.

The meeting between Troilus and Criseyde occurs inside the temple (scenes of happiness, as we will see, always occur within four walls). The narrator insists on the power of Criseyde's charms, with the repetition of terms related to the sense of sight. The terms reach their high point in the lines

> And of hire look in him ther gan to quyken
> So gret desir and such affeccioun,
> That in his herte botme gan to stiken
> Of hir his fixe and depe impressioun. (I, 295–8)

As in the stanza containing the mirror of the mind metaphor, Chaucer here adds elements from the *Filostrato* to the treatment of Criseyde's effect on Troilus, in order to examine it in greater depth. Criseyde arouses *desir* and *affeccioun* in him, and these are fitting sentiments for a young man who has fallen deeply in love with what his eyes have beheld.[15] Later, however, in the scene inside the room, the dominant

and Criseyde', in *Style and Consciousness in Middle English Narrative* (Princeton, 1983), pp. 79–102, and by J. Mann, 'Chance and Destiny in *Troilus and Criseyde* and the *Knight's Tale*', in P. Boitani and J. Mann, eds., *Cambridge Chaucer Companion*, pp. 75–92.

13 On the love-war relationship, see J. P. McCall, 'The Trojan Scene in Chaucer's *Troilus*', *English Literary History* 29 (1962) 263–75; on love as war, see the excellent essay, 'Mervelous Signals: Sign Theory and the Politics of Metaphor in Chaucer's *Troilus and Criseyde*', in E. Vance, *Mervelous Signals: Poetics and Sign Theory in the Middle Ages* (Lincoln and London, 1986), pp. 256–310, especially pp. 287–310.

14 On the characterization of Fortune in *Troilus and Criseyde*, see C. Wood, *The Elements of Chaucer's Troilus* (Durham, N.C., 1984), pp. 153–63, *passim*. The role of Fortune in Boethian terms is discussed at length by D. W. Robertson, Jr., *A Preface to Chaucer* (Princeton, 1962), pp. 472–503, *passim*.

15 On the Neoplatonic conception of the woman's face as a microcosm of beauty, cf. J. Frappier, 'Variations sur le thème du miroir, de Bernard de Ventadour à Maurice

isotopy in Troilus' reflection is *thought*. The intensity of his thought is such that his spirit longs to see the temple again, to recall the gaze Criseyde turned on him and to contemplate it once more: Troilus' love from its very onset becomes too private, idealized, and pervaded with the sense of death – as the last line of the *Canticus Troili* shows. The wholly inward movement that accompanies the various phases of love's growth reveals itself outwardly in the hero's renewed vigour in battle. The flame of love burning in Troilus' heart is converted into warlike deeds, while his love affair remains at a standstill within his mind.

At this point there appears another initiator of love affairs, Pandarus, who will 'construct' the actual meeting between the young man and woman.[16] Pandarus is well equipped to advise Troilus in matters of love, since, 'Sith thus of two contraries is o lore' (I, 645), he has experienced both the sweets and the pains of love. On Pandarus' lips the distinction between natural and spiritual love becomes a mere proverbial exemplification of knowing a thing by its opposite. Chaucer, therefore, unfolds the development of the story on two planes: the first is the province of the narrator, who 'knows' and intervenes at crucial moments with his apostrophes; the second is that of Pandarus, who reduces Troilus' complex love to earthly affection. Pandarus urges Troilus to tell him his lady's name, since he might know her. Like the narrator, Pandarus too is aware of the young man's strange attitude to love, but he attributes this peculiarity to Troilus' being half asleep and tells him to wake up. Troilus is not really asleep, because he hears what Pandarus is saying, but in his hopeless situation Pandarus' words are just empty to him.

A large part of Book I is based on this dichotomy – on one hand Pandarus' down-to-earth talk and on the other Troilus' intellectual speculations on love. This dichotomy is an instance of the deeper contrast that pervades the whole work, between the action and dynamism that characterize Pandarus and Criseyde, and the inaction that becomes transformed into intellectual frenzy in Troilus. Outside of this contrast there is the narrator continually underscoring the danger that looms over the young man. He does this with images associated with the

Scève', *Cahiers de l'Association Internationale des Études Françaises* 11 (1959) 134–58, especially pp. 151–2, and E. Köhler, 'Narcisse, la fontaine d'Amour et Guillaume de Lorris', *Journal des Savants* (Avril – Juin 1963) 86–103. On the symbolic functions of the heart, cf. S. L. Clark and J. N. Wasserman, 'The Heart in *Troilus and Criseyde*: The Eye of the Breast, the Mirror of the Mind, the Jewel in Its Setting', *Chaucer Review* 18 (1984) 316–28.

16 On Pandarus as 'operator', cf. Bishop, *Chaucer's Troilus and Criseyde*, pp. 32–42.

mirror metaphor, and synthesized iconographically in the changing wheel of Fortune and in the ladder.[17] The narrator declares that

> This Troilus is clomben on the staire,
> And litel weneth that he moot descenden;
> But alday faileth thing that fooles wenden. (I, 215–17)

He refers here to Troilus' pride when he showed himself contemptuous of love, and he also foreshadows Troilus' slow approach towards the earthly love by which he will be betrayed. Chaucer quite deliberately uses the ladder metaphor, since ladders have always been associated with the various stages of contemplation. Troilus uses the ladder improperly, because the object of contemplation cannot be love for a woman, especially for a woman who is *destined* to be faithless. The ladder is also a symbol of ascent towards something that cannot ever be wholly gained, and the ever-present images of death increase the sense of sorrow that pervades the songs and complaints of Troilus.

The risk inherent in the dark, veiled mirror of the world is exemplified at the end of Book I in the error Troilus commits by entrusting his ideals of life and death to Pandarus:

> But, thow wis, thow woost, thow maist, thow art al!
> My lif, my deth, hol in thyn hand I leye. (I, 1052–3)

With hyperbolical irony Troilus minimizes the values of his existence: previously the image of Criseyde was reflected in his mind; now his whole existence lies in Pandarus' hands. The hand of Pandarus may also stand for the hand of the poet rewriting the story, in which case Troilus' relinquishing his initiative to Pandarus may mean his entrusting himself to the author, who knows and understands everything about him – including his weakness. And it is precisely the understanding of Pandarus (or of the narrator) that allows Troilus to continue his 'adventure' and so pursue his inevitable destiny: 'And thus he dryeth forth his aventure' (I, 1092). Right from the start Troilus' progress towards love is hindered by obstacles and founded on a tragic misunderstanding. His adventure resembles a quest by which he believes that he is making a gradual approach to the knowledge of the highest good, but which will ultimately be revealed as the discovery of a betrayal.

17 For the link between the mirror image and the notion of the ladder, see Introduction, p. 21.

These observations on Troilus' behaviour might lead us to believe that Chaucer wanted to represent Criseyde, by way of contrast, as a woman given to treachery. In reality Book II's preparation for the physical fulfilment of love is preceded by an important self-justification by the narrator/poet; on the one hand he denies responsibility for the story, declaring himself no more than its translator from the Latin version; on the other, he acknowledges that manners and customs vary, in different countries and at different times.[18] The great pains he takes to disclaim responsibility correspond to the technique of self-depreciation, but before the disclaimer we have an impassioned invocation of the Muse and thus the recognition of his own function as poet, conscious of contructing something new and to the measure of the different society for which the text is destined. The frequency of the references to the *auctor* is explained by the narrator's distancing himself further and further from the 'matere' as the climax approaches. It also provides a means by which tragic and comic elements can be juxtaposed.

If Troilus were only a love-sick hero and the epitome of virtue, and Criseyde the female representation of Lust, one of the Seven Deadly Sins, we would have the makings of a morality play – and Pandarus would be a comical character. Chaucer's intention is not didactic – or at least it is not simply didactic – so that the Criseyde he gives us is a charming, intelligent young woman, in love with love even if, as Henryson was later to say, 'fortunait'.[19] The setting in which the meeting between Pandarus and Criseyde takes place is typical of the dream vision: it is May and Criseyde is reading a romance on the history of Thebes.[20] There is no need for us to go into the intricate parallels that have been drawn by various critics between the history of Thebes and that of Troy to show that the reference to tragic Thebes sounds as a presage of ill-fortune to the listener/reader. There is also an ominous reference to the story of Procne and Philomela: this story is a mirror, with the roles reversed, of Criseyde's betrayal of Troilus, since it was the man, Tereus, who was unfaithful in this case. Just when it would seem

18 See the beginning of Book II (ll. 1–49), where Chaucer states his role as a translator from Latin and emphasizes the natural changes that time and language are subjected to.

19 R. Henryson, *The Testament of Cresseid*, l. 79.

20 On the extensive use of the Theban history and legend made by Chaucer in the *Troilus*, see P. M. Clogan, 'The Theban Scenes in Chaucer's *Troilus*', *Medievalia et Humanistica* 12 (1984) 167–85, and W. Wetherbee, *Chaucer and the Poets. An Essay on Troilus and Criseyde* (Ithaca and London, 1984), especially pp. 111–44, where he states the importance of Statius and Dante's Statius for the *Troilus*.

that love is to be presented as a private matter, the indirect suggestion is made that it also has a public side. Criseyde's reading the *Thebaid* constitutes a reference to the tragic fate of the most famous city of antiquity after Troy itself, and the allusion to the conflict between Greeks and Trojans anticipates the imminent fall of Troy. The history of the war, interrupted for an account of Troilus' inner travail, is resumed with full force; it jolts the reader out of his involvement in the love-story which is being related, back to the larger state of affairs. Troilus and Criseyde are not just any two young people: they are Trojans, Troilus subject and Criseyde object within the ambit of the war.

The understatement represented by Pandarus in contrast to Troilus' idealism reappears in a further use of the mirror metaphor:

> And with that word he gan right inwardly
> Byholden hire and loken on hire face,
> And seyde, 'On swich a mirour goode grace!' (II, 264–6)

Unlike Troilus, Pandarus turns over in his mind ways and means of convincing Criseyde to go along with his plan, and he looks into his niece's eyes as he puts his admiration for her into words. There is a correspondence between the magnetic power of Troilus' mind and the entirely physical power of Pandarus' gaze: the former makes itself into a mirror to contain Criseyde's image and concentrates on identifying imagination with reality; the latter, accompanied by reassuring words, anticipates the happy outcome of his scheming. The analogy between Book I and II does not stop here, because in Book II there is also the repetition of Troilus' keyword *aventure*. Pandarus suggests that Criseyde surrender to the 'good aventure' (II, 288); he delivers a long tirade on the need to grasp good fortune at the right moment, thus playing on Criseyde's fearfulness. Pandarus goes so far as to make use of the *memento mori* commonplace associated with the mirror, which suggests the realistic detail of a Flemish picture:

> 'So longe mote ye lyve, and alle proude,
> Til crowes feet be growe under youre yë,
> And sende yow than a myrour in to prye,
> In which that ye may se youre face a morwe!' (II, 402–5)

This example anticipates the analogous exploitation of the mirror device in Henryson's *Testament* whereby Cresseid becomes conscious of the signs of the terrible disease of leprosy on her face.[21] The *memento mori* present in *Troilus* is thus transformed into Cresseid's actual death in the *Testament*.

The narrator underscores Criseyde's fear, piety, hesitancy and finally her capitulation out of curiosity. Criseyde's behaviour is rational and humanly aware that 'Of harmes two, the lesse is for to chese' (II, 470). After seeing Troilus at the height of his glory and being dazzled by him – 'Who yaf me drynke' (II, 651) – she defends her right to love and justifies it so long as honour and reputation are saved. Here too Chaucer intersperses the various speeches with forewarnings. The hendiadys in 'And kepe alwey myn honour and my name' (II, 762) stressing Criseyde's determination to remain true to her own ideals will reappear as a syntagma that Troilus pronounces in his desperation: 'Allas, youre name of trouthe / Is now fordon, and that is al my routhe' (V, 1686–7).

To return to structural parallels, what Troilus sees from the window is preceded by Pandarus' account of the supposed garden scene, and this is particularly tense with emotion because Criseyde has already decided to yield to love. There is a correspondence between the scene in Book I, where Troilus recalls Criseyde, and Book II, where Criseyde carefully evaluates Troilus' moral stature, his physique and his status: *prowesse, estat, renown, wit, shap, gentilesse* (II, 660–2). Her abandonment to the power of love, with Venus' favourable inclination to help Troilus,[22] does not make Criseyde forget the prudence necessary in her widowed state and in the absence of her father's protection. But her detailed examination of Troilus' value has been significantly placed by Chaucer after the question 'Who yaf me drynke?' (II, 651). Chaucer differentiates Criseyde's ability to love from Troilus', but he keeps within the bounds of plausibility the reaction of the young woman who, when her bewilderment has passed, reflects on the fate reserved for her. The key expression, 'But swich is love, and ek myn aventure' (II, 742), is repeated after Troilus is once more compared to Hector. Love springs naturally in the young woman's heart, but other contributing factors confirm her choice: Antigone's beautiful song[23] and, especially, Pandarus' intervention. At the end of Book II, Criseyde – 'Al innocent of Pandarus entente' (II,

[21] Cf. R. Henryson, *The Testament of Cresseid*, ll. 344–50.

[22] On Chaucer's treatment of Venus in the *Troilus*, see Wood, *The Elements of Chaucer's Troilus*, ch. IV.

[23] According to Sr. M. C. Borthwick, 'Antigone's Song as "Mirour" in Chaucer's *Troilus and Criseyde*', *Modern Language Quarterly* 22 (1961) 227–35, Antigone's song conveys the idea of insufficiency of human love and in so doing it reflects the attitudes towards love present in the poem.

1723) – takes her first steps towards the consummation of her love. Chaucer once more uses a double delaying tactic, consisting of a metanarrative by Pandarus urging the young woman to go to Troilus, and a narrative with the narrator's apostrophe to God. The excitement in Pandarus' voice that can be inferred from the terms associated with time intensifies the atmosphere of anxiety and uncertainty for the reader, while the narrator's question to God on the possible requests made in Troilus' prayer certainly allude to the final act, but also hint at the true end of Troilus' story, which is his death. Once more we have a feeling of uneasiness, due to the mention of sad mythological episodes at the moment of the two lovers' meeting – the history of Thebes, and the story of Procne and Philomela,[24] followed by the allusions in Troilus' speech to death and Fortune.

The audience that Chaucer is addressing – 'ye loveres that ben here' (II, 1751) – are like the narrator, already familiar with the plot, perhaps from their reading of Benoît and of Guido. As, however, the two possible ways of interpreting the history of Thebes show (Criseyde refers to the romance, Pandarus to Statius' *Thebaid*), the historical model can be reinterpreted so that it differs from the *auctoritas* (and we know that Chaucer *deviates* from the *Filostrato* and from Guido). What must remain intact are the two essential features of the story: Troilus must die, and Criseyde must by her betrayal bring about Troilus' death. The narrator/poet, who takes on only one episode of the complex history of Troy, is nevertheless within a tradition he cannot step outside of if he does not wish to lose his credibility as an *auctor*; but he is so securely within it that he feels himself personally involved. It could be argued that the narrator has a little of Criseyde in him when he smiles at Pandarus' games and when he delights in the lovers' happiness, and is to some extent Troilus when he introduces references to malevolent or uncertain destiny.

Book III is central to Troilus and Criseyde's love relationship. The structural elements of this book are the opening and closing hymns to Venus – both as planet and goddess of love – the purpose of which is to underscore the lovers' happiness. On a close examination, the first hymn appears to be very ambiguous in its intertextual reference. The line 'In gentil hertes ay redy to repaire' (III, 5), attributed to Venus, certainly echoes the famous first line of Guinizelli's Canzone, 'Al cor

24 On the myth of Procne and Philomela, see Wetherbee, *Chaucer and the Poets*, pp. 154–8.

gentil rimpaira sempre Amore'. Furthermore, the relationship between love and 'gentilesse' is also present in Dante's Sonnet in the *Vita Nuova*, 'A ciascun'alma presa e gentil core' (III) and in *Inferno* V, 100, 'Amor, ch'al cor gentil ratto s'apprende' – within the Paolo and Francesca episode, thus uniting two very different women, Beatrice and Francesca, under the same conception of love.[25] In using a line so full of reminiscences, Chaucer, the narrator, tries to distance himself from the two lovers in the very moment in which he brings them together, thus giving the reader another clue to the coming sorrow. At the end of the proem, there is a new disturbing echo from Dante (*Paradiso* XXXIII, 16), when Venus is referred to almost as the Virgin Mary (III, 39). In this way Chaucer is reinforcing the validity of natural love through the supreme example of the mother of God. The emphasis on the pagan and 'Christian' elements in Venus and on the virtuous and sinful aspects of love through Beatrice and Francesca anticipates Troilus' idea of love as both a physical and mental experience, but one which is mainly felt as a state of mind.

The scene of the fulfilment of the lovers' desire is studded with ominous allusions. The use of the image of the dying man who succeeds in coming back to life from an incurable disease repeats the associations Troilus has already made between love and death. The dominant motif of the merging of natural and supernatural reappears when the delicate description of Criseyde's physical beauty is placed alongside the invocation to Venus:

> Than seyde he thus, 'O Love, O Charite!
> Thi moder ek, Citheria the swete,
> After thiself next heried be she –
> Venus mene I, the wel-willy planete! –
> And next that, Imeneus, I the grete;
> For nevere man was to yow goddes holde
> As I, which ye han brought fro cares colde. (III, 1254–60)

Within this stanza lies the contradiction that Troilus endeavours to resolve: as an ideal pagan knight he has, as part of his make-up, the inclination towards sensual love and its fulfilment, but as a *persona* created by the poet he embodies consciousness of the conventions governing amorous sentiment. Natural love is equated with 'charite', and

25 On Chaucer as a reader of Dante, see K. Taylor, 'A Text and Its Afterlife: Dante and Chaucer', *Comparative Literature* 35 (1983) 1–20.

the prayer to Venus is extended to Hymen, the divinity presiding over marriage. The knight Troilus at the service of war and love[26] takes on a quality which, while it cannot be called Christian, is the closest a pagan can get to being so. Love, as we have learnt, implies total commitment for Troilus: it involves senses and mind, feeling and reason. The erotic element is not lacking, but it is recombined and sublimated by the rational awareness of love as a social tie. This meaning of love reappears when Troilus expresses wonder at feeling himself bound without bonds – 'How koude ye withouten bond me bynde?' (III, 1358)[27] – and when the narrator describes the exchange of rings by the two lovers: 'And pleyinge entrechaungeden hire rynges' (III, 1368). The verb *entrechaungeden* takes up the greater part of the line with its threatening length, almost as if to allude to the other meaning of 'exchange' it includes.[28] The exchanging of rings, which almost suggests a secret wedding, is the first of an unhappy series of exchanges: Antenor is exchanged for Criseyde and Troilus is exchanged for Diomede.

The narrator expresses the difficulty he has in speaking about love to an audience of experienced lovers:

> For myne wordes, heere and every part,
> I speke hem alle under correccioun
> Of yow that felyng han in loves art,
> And putte it al in youre discrecioun
> To encresse or maken dymynucioun
> Of my langage, and that I yow biseche. (III, 1331–6)

This difficulty finds an echo in the metaphor of Troilus' confession that he cannot read what is in Criseyde's heart:

> Though ther be mercy writen in youre cheere,
> God woot, the text ful hard is, soth, to fynde! (III, 1356–7)

On the one hand these two lines express Troilus' joy at having won Criseyde – a prize that has cost him effort and that is his by love's

26 On Troilus as both warrior and lover, see M. Storm, 'Troilus, Mars, and Late Medieval Chivalry', *Journal of Medieval and Renaissance Studies* 12 (1982) 45–65, and Wood, *The Elements of Chaucer's Troilus*, especially pp. 38–98.

27 The various meanings of the bondage of love are analysed by S. A. Barney, 'Troilus Bound', *Speculum* 47 (1972) 445–58.

28 On marriage as a kind of economic exchange in the Late Middle Ages, see S. Medcalf, ed., *The Later Middle Ages* (London, 1981), pp. 231–43.

miracle; on the other hand, on the narratorial plane, they are a metalinguistic representation of a heightened consciousness, the consciousness of the difficulty involved in 'finding the text' and in giving readers a plausible version of it in relation to the courtly poetry they are familiar with.[29] At the same time the poet makes a great effort to interpret such 'classic' subject-matter in a new way, in a different situation. Chaucer's insistence on metalinguistic metaphors is another strong signal of the strange relationship he has with his 'matere', which combines involvement and distance. The narrator's sympathetic attitude – and in this he is the opposite of Pandarus, who eggs the lovers on – is revealed in his delicate handling of the various phases of the lovers' consummation of desire, while the sense of his keeping his distance is given not only by frequent irony, but also, and in particular, by the stress laid on Troilus' existential 'failure to understand'. Troilus' idealism, which seems to place his service to his beloved above all other social relations, is in reality the product of medieval society, in which marriage and family ties were becoming increasingly important. From his knowledge of the impossibility of the lovers' being permanently united the narrator introduces yet another component, which we might define as narcissistic, into Troilus' conception of love.[30] This component can be inferred from Troilus' aspiration to embrace Criseyde's whole person in Book I, but it is made quite clear when the lovers must part after their first night of love. Like the practical person she is, Criseyde reminds Troilus that he must go, because dawn is breaking and time is running out; he shows by his behaviour that he considers love one of the fundamental things of life – which, however, is made up also of social relations. Criseyde displays this rational side to her character from the very beginning when, deserted by Calchas, she asks Hector for his protection – and she also displays it when in the end she betrays Troilus for Diomede. Circumstances have

29 On the audience of the *Troilus*, see D. Mehl, 'The Audience of Chaucer's *Troilus and Criseyde*', in *Chaucer and Middle English Studies in Honour of Rossell Hope Robbins*, ed. B. Rowland (London, 1974), pp. 173–89, and P. Strohm, 'Chaucer's Audience(s): Fictional, Implied, Intended, Actual', *Chaucer Review* 18 (1983) 137–45. See also Strohm's *Social Chaucer* (Cambridge, Mass. and London, 1989), pp. 55–64.

30 The destructive power of self-love is shown in the *Roman de la Rose*, where the Narcissus story plays a central role: cf. Köhler, 'Narcisse, la fontaine d'Amour et Guillaume de Lorris'. On the influence of the episode in the *Troilus*, see Wood, *The Elements of Chaucer's Troilus*, pp. 79–80, and for a Freudian interpretation, cf. D. B. Wilson, 'The Commerce of Desire: Freudian Narcissism in Chaucer's *Troilus and Criseyde* and Shakespeare's *Troilus and Cressida*', *English Language Notes* 20 (1983) 11–22.

forced Criseyde to fend for herself, and for this reason her love affair, which gives her a valiant man by her side, is also a source of protection and reassurance for her. Troilus' love is even more cerebral than it is physical, creating a division within his heart.

Corresponding to Criseyde's 'That day of us moot make dissever-aunce!' (III, 1424) – where *us* is clear evidence of her awareness of duality in the love relationship – is Troilus' variant: 'Now fele I that myn herte moot a-two' (III, 1475). Here, by way of stressing once more the absolute nature of his love, it is *his* heart that splits into two. Troilus' unhappiness seems similar to that of Narcissus, who, since he identifies himself with his lover, dies of a surfeit of love. Unlike Narcissus, however, Troilus does not love himself: he loves a flesh and blood woman, but his love is too comtemplative. As such it is in conflict with reality, which, once it becomes known to him, will prove fatal. This important stage in their love is marked by another image of the mind as a mirror. That progress has been made is quite certain: love as pure desire, the form it took after the scene in the temple, reaches its fulfilment; but important as this physical consummation is, it does not seem to have modified Troilus' narcissistic attitude to any great extent since, once back in his palace, he gives himself up to reflection on what Criseyde said and on the way she looked:

> And in his thought gan up and down to wynde
> Hire wordes alle, and every countenaunce,
> And fermerly impressen in his mynde
> The leeste point that to him was plesaunce;
> And verraylich of thilke remembraunce
> Desir al newe hym brende, and lust to brede
> gan more than erst, and yet took he non hede. (III, 1541–7)

In the final words, 'yet took he non hede', lies all Troilus' passivity. The love song after Boethius that closes Book III is a hymn to the harmony that reigns in the universe, a harmony that reconciles and embodies opposites, and admits of change. In reality the narrator's reference to the war and Troilus' valour destroys this harmony by introducing the motif of discord. The change Criseyde is subjected to does not come about only because of the state of flux in Nature and the fickleness of womankind, but above all because of the pressure of public circumstances; the exchange of Antenor for Criseyde is authorized for reasons arising out of the war, and this will part the lovers. Troilus' idea of the unity of natural and spiritual is impossible for him to achieve, because Troilus is not Dante, and because the outside world exercises its authority. The war that Chaucer has deliberately excluded by referring his readers to other versions of the history of Troy is nonetheless present and looms over Troilus' future.

Book IV opens with the image of Fortune's wheel and ends with Criseyde's premonition of a dire fate: 'And this may lengthe of yeres naught fordo, / Ne remuable Fortune deface' (IV, 1681–2). In the proem the narrator seems to intend leaving Criseyde to her fate. His sympathetic attitude to her seems to vanish, cancelled out by the directness of the line, 'For how Criseyde Troilus forsook' (IV, 15), then modified in tone by 'Or at the leeste, how that she was unkynde' (IV, 16). With this weak, unstressed adjective Chaucer attenuates Criseyde's guilt, for which he had already adduced several excuses. Troilus is present when the decision is taken to exchange Criseyde for Antenor: in desperation he first tries to think of a way of saving Criseyde's honour and then of avoiding the exchange. Paradoxically it is Hector who, in defence of Criseyde's liberty, hints at her future faithlessness in the declaration, 'We usen here no wommen for to selle' (IV, 182). Hector's proud claim has no effect, because – among other things – the Trojans are not so loyal and generous as might be thought. A war waged abroad has been brought home by the abduction of Helen, and Criseyde's exchange for Antenor will mean Troilus' death, but also the end of Troy.[31] When weighed against each other, Criseyde's personal betrayal will prove of little account in relation to Antenor's.

Troilus gives vent to his desperation in the bedroom that witnessed his flights of fancy and his happiness. Where in Book I his mind had reflected the image of Criseyde, now Troilus himself becomes

> Ful lik a ded ymage, pale and wan; (IV, 235)

This is a reference to the *Aeneid* and the *Inferno*, but certainly also to the vain images that Boethius speaks of (*Boece* V, m. 4, 26). Criseyde's imminent departure eliminates the possibility of Troilus' reflecting her beauty and transforms Troilus into a vain image. The mirror metaphor has been almost fully exploited: Troilus' mind has acted as a mirror

[31] The connection between the war *within* and the war *without* constitutes the main attraction for the poets – and Chaucer among them – who deal with the archetype of Troy's fall: cf. E. Vance, 'Mervelous Signals: Poetics, Sign Theory, and Politics in Chaucer's *Troilus*', *New Literary History* 10 (1979) 293–337, pp. 299–303.

reflecting Ideal Beauty in the contingent body of Criseyde, and this same mind has narcissistically loved the object of its own ideal reflection, almost forgetting its corporeal element. What remains to be seen is the mirror in its ideal form and to appreciate its intrinsic value, and this characteristic of the mirror can be grasped only when the things of this world have been left behind. Troilus feels that he can do nothing to oppose destiny, and his apostrophe to Fortune is an acknowledgement of his impotence to do so. Troilus and Criseyde's *aventure* has already been transformed into 'This infortune or this disaventure' (IV, 297). In the face of this sad quirk of fate nothing remains for Troilus but to die – 'But ende I wol, as Edippe, in derknesse / My sorwful lif, and dyen in distresse' (IV, 300–1) – since eyes deprived of the light shining from Criseyde no longer have any reason to 'see'. The mixture of natural and supernatural previously noted is evident in Troilus' failure to come to grips with his fate: once more the over-intellectualization of love leads him to imagine the suffering he foresees but cannot know. Instead of acting, of opposing the parliament's decision, he complains and compares himself to unhappy Oedipus, thus making a further connection with the history of Thebes. By associating Troilus' story with the tragedy of Oedipus (even if it is an exaggeration to do so), Chaucer once again links Troilus' end and the public destiny of Troy. Above all he underscores the blindness of Troilus' behaviour. From the very start he has made a wrong use of his eyes to see the beauty of Criseyde's flesh as an image of Eternal Beauty, to the point of associating eros with charity in the invocation he pronounces on the occasion of his love's physical consummation. His seeing the Ideal in Criseyde proves to be an illusion, however, since the Ideal suddenly escapes him when he has to take account of reality. If Criseyde were indeed the being descended from heaven to earth to show the greatness of divine love, then Troilus would not need eyes to see, because her image would have always been impressed on his mind. But he has been blind from the start, because he has not known how to be content with the natural human element in that love.[32]

The poet's great ability lies in his giving Troilus a hint of what motivations bring about his inevitable fate, without making his foresighted wisdom weigh too heavily and without attributing to Criseyde

32 The motif of blindness and pride which is present in the Oedipus story reminds the reader of the close relationship between the fate of Thebes and the fate of Troy, but at the same time it connects Troilus' attitude towards love with the Narcissus story by way of Tiresias' prophecy ('Si se non noverit'). Narcissus' perilous mirror of self-love becomes Troilus' personal fate which is in turn the symbol of Troy's fall.

sole responsibility for the betrayal. Step by step, even without his being aware of it, Troilus acquires a germ of understanding, as when he argues that Criseyde is superior 'To creature yformed here by kynde' (IV, 451), and when he expresses the wish to die and go to the Underworld with Proserpina. The allusion to Proserpina is an important one because of the association with abduction, a compelling issue in Troy.[33] Troilus, true to an abstract conception of honour, lets Criseyde be exchanged for Antenor and in so doing allows the Trojans to bring about the fall of Troy. When Pandarus suggests the lovers' flight as a possible solution, Troilus proudly declares:

> First, syn thow woost this town hath al this werre
> For ravysshyng of wommen so by myght,
> It sholde nought be suffred me to erre,
> As it stant now, ne don so gret unright.
> I sholde han also blame of every wight,
> My fadres graunt if that I so withstoode,
> Syn she is chaunged for the townes goode. (IV, 547–53)

When Troilus speaks about the ravishing of women in the plural he is alluding to the first of the series of abductions that have led up to Criseyde's being sent to the Greek camp. Hesione, Priam's sister, was given by Heracles to Telamon after the first destruction of Troy. Seeing that the Greeks do not intend giving her back, Paris, who has fallen in love with Helen, causes the war by abducting her and bringing her back with him to Troy. Troilus behaves like the other Trojans when he lets Criseyde go, because by so doing he joins them in using women as goods for barter. Troilus sacrifices Criseyde to the good of the city and the will of his father.

The harmony of natural and supernatural that he believed he had achieved is shattered in the following stanza:

> Thus am I lost, for aught that I kan see.
> For certeyn is, syn that I am hire knyght,
> I moste hire honour levere han than me
> In every cas, as lovere ought of right.
> Thus am I with desir and reson twight:

[33] For a comparison between the myth of Proserpina and Pluto and the story of Troilus and Criseyde, see Rowe, *O Love O Charite!*, pp. 131–2.

Desir for to destourben hire me redeth,
And reson nyl nat; so myn herte dredeth. (IV, 568–74)

The first part of this passage stresses the knight's duty to treasure above all else his lady's honour, as befits a perfect lover; the second part speaks openly of the discord embedded in the apparent harmony of honour and courtly love, of whose presence Troilus is slowly becoming convinced. The striking chiastic structure that Lydgate was to use so aptly in *variatio* form for the lady's speech in the *Temple of Glas*[34] reveals Troilus' inner conflict. The chiastic structure requires that to *desir* should correspond the dread in his heart and that *reson* should guide Troilus in preventing Criseyde from being sent to the Greek camp. In time of war there is no room either for Hector's disinterested justice or for Troilus' wishes. The good of the nation requires that reason smother aspirations. Once again Troilus' idealism runs up against hard reality.

Criseyde hears news of the exchange but does not dare to confide in anyone 'for fere' (IV, 672).[35] Chaucer makes a point of Criseyde's fearfulness to justify her despair and her feeling of being deserted. Criseyde, a natural being whose love lacks a spiritual dimension, describes her new state, in animal- and vegetable-related metaphors, in terms of goods for barter:

To what fyn sholde I lyve and sorwen thus?
How sholde a fissh withouten water dure?
What is Criseyde worth, from Troilus?
How sholde a plaunte or lyves creature
Lyve withouten his kynde noriture?
For which ful ofte a by-word here I seye,
That 'rooteles moot grene soone deye.' (IV, 764–70)

Chaucer gives Criseyde the words that link her to the narrator: 'To what fyn sholde I lyve and sorwen thus?'. Criseyde is unable to understand the reasons behind the exchange, because her behaviour has always been dictated by feeling, and the narrator would like to be ignorant of the ending towards which the story must necessarily move from this point on. Criseyde gives expression in her monologue to her awareness of the end of earthly happiness: 'Endeth than love in wo? Ye, or men lieth, /

34 See chapter II.
35 The theme of fear in *Troilus and Criseyde* is treated extensively by Minnis, *Chaucer and Pagan Antiquity*, pp. 93–107.

And alle worldly blisse, as thynketh me!' (IV, 834–5). Man is nothing in the face of Fortune's and the planets' power – a plaything to be tossed about by forces greater than himself. Criseyde will not accept Pandarus' consoling words: there is nothing now that can mend her situation. Even her face, the mirror of beauty and happiness, changes, and this physical change precedes a moral one:

> Hire face, lik of Paradys the ymage,
> Was al ychaunged in another kynde. (IV, 864–5)

The association of 'Paradys' and 'another kynde' gives us the sense of Criseyde's degeneration as a character and by extension the degeneration of the love story. And yet the same metaphor with a simple *variatio* in Book V, 817 – 'Paradis stood formed in hire yën', loses its negative connotation to re-acquire its meaning in the light of the *dolce stil novo* doctrine. Criseyde will soon betray Troilus for Diomede, but the narrator cannot help admiring her almost heavenly beauty. Nevertheless the nearness of the metaphor to the moment of the betrayal suggests that Criseyde's beauty is earthly, therefore fallible. The long philosophical monologue that Troilus pronounces on the necessity of human events ('For al that comth, comth by necessitee' – IV, 958) derives from Boethius, but it is also the final outcome of the complex psychological scrutiny provided by the narrator. If on the one hand the argument is an expression of the philosophical speculation current in Chaucer's time, to make it come from Troilus' lips is to answer the need to stress the contemplative nature of this character.[36] When the events of the world around him take charge and determine the course of his affections, Troilus – who has experienced love as a mental state whose physical expression, due to Pandarus' intervention, seems almost incidental – takes refuge in a determinism aimed at justifying his inaction. Assuming that everything occurs of necessity, this fatalistic necessity, supernatural in nature, is preceded, as Chaucer has pointed out, by Troilus' speech to Pandarus, a speech in which he denies the possibility of modifying the order given by the parliament in the name of another kind of necessity. The necessity Troilus seems to obey is first and foremost that of state and family, although this does not exclude *a priori* his freedom to act differ-

[36] On Troilus as a 'fatalistic lover' and a 'fatalistic philosopher', see again Minnis, *Chaucer and Pagan Antiquity*, pp. 93–107.

ently. Notwithstanding this, however, the narrator has presented the reader with a Troilus in thrall to ineluctable forces.

At first derisive of love, Troilus becomes blinded by love of Criseyde in Book I and then, almost against his will, he is put into Criseyde's bed to enjoy the sweets of love in forgetfulness of his royal rank. Unlike Hector, who endeavours to oppose the parliament's decision, Troilus accepts it as inevitable. His considerations on necessity are therefore the final result of this characterization of Troilus, which once more stresses the metaphysical element in his love. Criseyde's reaction is in sharp contrast to Troilus' bowing to fate. Such is the depth of her love that she first swoons and almost dies of sorrow; she then takes the situation in hand and insists, without wasting time – 'For which I wol nat make long sermoun – / For tyme ylost may nought recovered be – / But I wol gon to my conclusioun' (IV, 1282–4) – on putting forward as the only solution that she should leave for the Greek camp and return within ten days. The exclusively temporal dimension that Criseyde brings her love down to is in sharp contrast with Troilus' idealization, but it is also an anticipation of the reasons for the betrayal to which she is about to descend. Time, which inevitably puts an end to all things – and which has already written *finis* to the lovers' brief union – seems to be underestimated in Criseyde's speech.

An atmosphere of ambiguity and improbability is created by Criseyde's words. Her allusion to the chances of peace being declared on Helen's return to the Greek camp is rendered unconvincing by the reference that follows to the certainty of Calchas' letting Criseyde return to Troy. If Calchas has begged to have his daughter back with him it is because he knows that Troy's fate is about to be sealed; on the other hand, the highlighting of Calchas' *cupiditas* serves only to increase the sense of impending doom. The irony of what Criseyde is saying is seen in synthesis in the line, 'I shal hym so enchaunten with my sawes' (IV, 1395). The allusion is to Criseyde's power to spellbind men with her gaze, and it is a foreshadowing of Diomede's power to enchant the young woman with his linguistic role-playing – his hypocritical deployment of the language of love. This premonition can be found in Troilus' speech, where he warns Criseyde of the spellbinding power of language: 'He shal som Grek so preyse and wel alose, / That ravysshen he shal yow with his speche' (IV, 1473–4). Troilus trembles at the thought that Criseyde's plan may not be put into effect, but Criseyde tries to convince him with a series of vows to the very gods whose credibility she has previously questioned. She adds a further element to the necessity for her to leave by putting *her* life and Troilus' honour on the same plane, thus proving her ability to exploit the power of language. Since she is aware that Troilus pursues abstract ideals, she justifies her departure with those ideals of courtly love, *honour* and *honeste*, that are about to be trodden underfoot as empty meaningless names.[37] The recognition of fate's necessity is transformed here by Criseyde into a simple moral exhortation: 'Thus maketh vertu of necessite' (IV, 1586).

Criseyde's profession of eternal faithfulness rings ironically in the ears of the reader who knows the outcome of the story, an outcome which is almost anticipated by the association of *trouthe* with *morwe* in 'Or here my trouthe: I wol naught lyve tyl morwe' (IV, 1617): Criseyde will not stay faithful for long once she is in the Greek camp. Criseyde may have been sincere when she declared that the quality that most attracted her to Troilus was his moral virtue (IV, 1672–3), but it is also true that it is faithfulness which will be lacking in her.

Book V opens with various forewarnings of Troy's end, from the invocation to the Fates to the readiness with which Diomede agrees to accompany Criseyde. A sense of Criseyde's definite exclusion from Troy is given by the repetition of *out of a town* (V, 21) and by *at the yate* (V, 32). At the moment of parting Criseyde sighs and goes forward. The narrator comments:

> There is non other remedie in this cas.
> And forth she rit ful sorwfully a pas.
> What wonder is, though that hire sore smerte,
> When she forgoth hire owen swete herte? (V, 60–3)

These lines too need to be read on two levels: on one there is the inevitability of Criseyde's betrayal of Troilus, on the other the impossibility for the narrator to deviate from the path beaten by the *auctores*. Criseyde must go to the Greek camp and Troilus 'to Troie homward' (V, 91). Criseyde remains within Troy in so far as she remains in Troilus' heart, but in spatial and temporal reality she is outside it. The separation in space and time that might, however, be overcome by the oneness of spirit that Troilus deludes himself he will be able to keep intact, is rendered insuperable by the closure that the words of Criseyde's letter hint at. Troilus had accused his sister of witchcraft when she had ended

37 The 'inter-relatedness' of the moral and aesthetic values in the poem is clearly demonstrated by A. Lockhart, 'Semantic, Moral, and Aesthetic Degeneration in *Troilus and Criseyde*', *Chaucer Review* 8 (1973) 100–18.

her interpretation of his dream with the unequivocal line, 'This Diomede is inne, and thow art oute' (V, 1519): now at last he understands. The final conclusion of the story comes at the moment when Troilus sees the tangible evidence of Criseyde's treachery – the *brooch*. It is interesting to see how Chaucer at this point ends Troilus and Criseyde's love story with a reversal of the mirror image in Book I. The stanza at the beginning of the first Book and the one at the end of Book V are a symmetrical representation of the whole mental process of love as Troilus conceives it. In both the mind makes a mirror of itself, in Book I to enclose the beloved's reflection, in Book V to exclude it. The two stanzas also act as a mirror in that they both reflect for the reader an image of Troilus' love as seen from the narrator's point of view. Finally, they reflect each other by means of the same or mirroring terms.

In sum, they are evidence of the poet's deliberate use of the mirror. Analogies and differences in his use of this metaphor become apparent upon detailed analysis:

> Thus gan he make a mirour of his mynde,
> In which he saugh al holly hire figure,
> And that he wel koude in his herte fynde.
> It was to hym a right good aventure
> To love swich oon, and if he dede his cure
> To serven hir, yet myghte he falle in grace,
> Or ellis for oon of hire servantz pace. (I, 365–71)

> Thorugh which I se that clene out of youre mynde
> Ye han me cast – and I ne kan nor may,
> For al this world, withinne myn herte fynde
> To unloven yow a quarter of a day!
> In corsed tyme I born was, weilaway,
> That yow, that doon me al this wo endure,
> Yet love I best of any creature! (V, 1695–701)

In the first stanza it is the narrator who describes the working of Troilus' memory, while in the second Troilus himself realizes that Criseyde has deserted him. This change in point of view is basic to Chaucer's interpretation of the Troilus story, because it sums up its *a quo* and *ad quem* aspects. By contact with reality, the natural and spiritual love that Troilus felt for Criseyde after his visit to the temple has gradually – during the course of the narration and by the narrator's direct intervention – been split into its two component parts: on the one hand,

Criseyde's conception of love has always represented the natural pole, on the other Troilus' love has always been characterized as more ideal and spiritual, even while it is being physically consummated.

It should be noted that the same terms appear in the second stanza as in the first, but they are here given negative characteristics: *mirour of his mynde* → *out of youre mynde*; *he saugh al holly hire figure* → *I se . . . Ye han me cast*; *he wel koude in his herte fynde* → *I ne kan nor may, . . . withinne myn herte fynde*; *To love swich oon* → *To unloven yow*. This use of the mirror metaphor is clearly a most sophisticated one: in the first case Troilus' mind is a positive mirror, reflecting as it does his idea of love; in the second Criseyde's mind, as Troilus sees it, is an empty mirror, because it no longer reflects love for him. The mirror of Criseyde's mind now acts like a material earthly object, deprived even of memory of her lover. According to Troilus, Criseyde has wiped out even the memory of her love for him. As Criseyde's mind, however, alludes by antithesis to the mind/mirror of Troilus, for the very reason that it has a negative value it allows him to *see* the truth. Criseyde has betrayed him, and he will love her for ever. Troilus' self-awareness is marked by a change of language: terms like *aventure*, *serven*, *grace*, *servantz*, which are of courtly derivation, are replaced with words having to do with earthly time (*a quarter of a day*, *in corsed tyme*), with unhappiness on earth (*al this wo*), and with the earthly sphere to which he recognizes his love for Criseyde belongs: *Yet love I best of any creature*. By laying stress on the temporal element the 'natural' change in Criseyde is pointed up. For Troilus Criseyde's letter is 'a kalendes of chaunge' (V, 1634) foreshadowing the bitter realization: 'Allas, I nevere wolde han wend, er this, / That ye, Criseyde, koude han chaunged so' (V, 1682–3). This change in Criseyde is made clear in terms of choice of words by her favourite refrain *trouthe*/*routhe* being repeated. The *trouthe* she was so proud of in Book IV – for which she was ready to die – is *now* revealed in Troilus' eyes as a mere 'name of trouthe' (V, 1686), and Criseyde's *routhe* for Troilus is transformed into Troilus' inconsolable complaint: 'and that is al my routhe' (V, 1687).

Criseyde's betrayal of Troilus takes place, therefore, on both the natural and the ideal plane: the *brooch* that signifies remembrance of Troilus is given to Diomede almost as if to set a tangible seal on an exchange that also involves her affections; Criseyde erases the memory of Troilus from her mind when, 'for despit' (V, 1693) she presents Diomede with precisely that *sign*. To a certain extent Criseyde's guilt is attenuated by this insistence on the change that has occurred in her, which brings to mind the exchange of Criseyde for Antenor dictated by political expediency. Now that he has come to the end of his story the narrator *must* admit Criseyde's faithlessness. As he has told his tale, Chaucer – by interspersing it with narratorial comment – has tried to show us the objective conditions that would lead to Criseyde's being unfaithful: he has also put his finger on Troilus' attitude to love as a possible cause of a *necessary* disappointment. He received his story from the *auctores* and he is bound to respect historical verisimilitude in his approach to a pagan world that is distant and yet, because of the mythical descent of England from Troy, near. Within the limitations imposed by these factors the narrator analyses the two main characters and the 'creator' of the story, Pandarus (his double), and he shows us the many-sided nature of their psyches so that we can better understand their actions and the final outcome that these *must* lead to. The problem of love, then, of *fyn lovynge*, is bound up with the problem of composing poetry, of narration. For Chaucer true love is closely tied to faithfulness, since fidelity in earthly love (*trouthe*) can reflect eternal fidelity (*Trouthe*). But this is only one aspect of the problems that are interwoven in the poem. The attraction of the love story of Troilus and Criseyde lies in the relationship of Troy to the rise of the European nations, providing as it did a rich source of subject-matter for the vernacular languages that were developing. Certainly Chaucer, the first poet to write solely and extensively in English, was not immune to its attraction.[38] A theme such as unfaithfulness or betrayal has a historical reason for its widespread circulation: the breach of faith, the breaking of an ideal bond, presupposes the irruption of time, of finiteness, of limitation into timelessness, infinitude, boundlessness, all of which formed part of the ideal conception of love.[39]

Chaucer feels limited by his 'matere' in the handling of such an archetypal subject, but he is also reassured by the likeness that the present evils bear to those of the past. The resemblances between Priam's and Richard II's court are indeed striking. What joins present to past and gives a foresight of the future is change, which does not only mean betrayal but also the mere, natural evolution of the seasons, the natural change in language, and the inconstant nature of human beings

[38] The influence of the legend of Troy on the 'political imagination of Europe' is shown by Vance, *Mervelous Signals*, pp. 264–9.

[39] On betrayal as a fascinating subject for Chaucer's time, see D. Kelly, *Medieval Imagination. Rhetoric and the Poetry of Courtly Love* (Madison and London, 1978), pp. 195–203.

that can at times lead to betrayal. Chaucer himself is in a certain sense guilty of betrayal in his translation, his reworking of such a well-known story. He has not only betrayed Criseyde by helping to hand down to future generations a dishonourable image of her, but he has also betrayed the *auctores* by telling the story in English, a different language, and by choosing to recount only the love story (even though in the context of the war). But given that language and style change in the course of time and in different contexts – as the use of English instead of French or Latin shows – what story could better be reworked by Chaucer than that of Troilus and Criseyde, based as it is on change itself? On the other hand, consciousness of the passing of time and impending death permeates late medieval English literature, so that a story that ends with the hero's death caters to this taste.

Every reading of *Troilus and Criseyde* offers new insights into its innumerable facets. Chaucer's almost obsessive search for new forms of expression – that must not however break with tradition – had often led him to set aside his works before they were finished (see, for example, the *House of Fame*). In *Troilus and Criseyde* this search, if it is not brought to its final conclusion, is at least brought to a possible conclusion. The fact of having tried his hand at all the literary genres available makes Chaucer realize that he is entitled to place the fruits of his labours among the immortals – Virgil, Homer, Lucan, Ovid, and Statius – and among the new classical authors whom he does not nominate but who serve as models for him – Dante, Petrarch, Boccaccio. Alongside the self-consciousness of his own worth as poet and of the dignity of his poem – open to correction though it may be by the 'moral Gower' and the 'philosophical Strode' – there is his serious preoccupation with the difficulty of his undertaking. Like the great writers of the past and present, Chaucer makes the effort to transform an oft-told tale into a *unique* work, and he continually gives his reader explanations of his method, even to the extent of addressing the reader directly in the very last book:

> Thow, redere, maist thiself ful wel devyne
> That swich a wo my wit kan nat diffyne;
> On ydel for to write it sholde I swynke,
> Whan that my wit is wery it to thynke. (V, 270–3)

With the usual *diminutio* technique Chaucer declares that he cannot describe Troilus' grief. But he uses terms – *diffyne, write, thynke* – that refer precisely to the process of writing which is going on in front of his eyes and those of the hypothetical future *redere* with whom the narrator and Pandarus have conversed throughout the poem. The dramatic (and I use this term in its strict sense) 'Thow maist' unites the two kinds of audience Chaucer imagines: on the one hand the young members of the court whom he has often addressed as they listen to *Troilus* being read aloud, on the other the future generations who will read the poem and – with due reservations as regards to the changes in manners and tastes of any particular time – who will be satisfied by it. Chaucer's reference to the reader at this point also serves to remind him that the story that has been told is a story of grief and woe. Not that Chaucer wants to retract anything that he has said up to that moment: right from the beginning the narrator has been explicit about the 'tragic' nature of Troilus' story. His insistence on the difficulty he finds in expressing human grief and suffering, however, allows the reader to realize that the mixture of earthly and spiritual, of human and divine, that formed Troilus' conception of love on earth is to be avoided because it is mistaken and leads to disaster. By referring to the reader, Chaucer shatters any possible illusion about a hypothetical happy ending to the love story on earth, illusion created in the course of the tale. The references to the reader, to the 'litel bok' and to the 'yonge, fresshe folkes' (V, 1835) shift the attention back to the here and now with an abrupt swing from the pagan past to the reality of the Christian present. Only after his death, when he has ascended to the eighth sphere, can Troilus really see ('with ful avysement' – 1811) the harmony of the universe and be aware at last of the supreme *Trouthe* that governs all things, alongside which his love for Criseyde is nothing more than a faded, botched copy. And it is precisely at this moment that the Pauline metaphor of the mirror is informed with truth by the narrator's directing the young audience to the one example of true fusion between divine and human: God in the Trinity.[40] Specularity disappears and the 'likeness' or 'image' of man to God found in Genesis is the *only* important relationship. The exhortation

> And of youre herte up casteth the visage
> To thilke God that after his ymage
> Yow made . . . (V, 1838–40)

[40] The emphasis on various forms of *seeing* in the *Troilus* is explained by L. Tarte Holley, 'Medieval Optics and the Framed Narrative in Chaucer's *Troilus and Criseyde*', *Chaucer Review* 21 (1986) 26–44, in terms of the medieval interest in optics.

finally solves the dramatic dilemma that Troilus, the narrator and the reader have been caught up in: earthly love, which is in itself good, is subject to betrayal and faithlessness, because of the 'false worldes brotelnesse' (V, 1832) for which 'the forme of olde clerkis speche / In poetrie' (V, 1854–5) often serves as vehicle. True love, however, is divine love. Christ 'nyl falsen no wight, . . . / That wol his herte al holly on hym leye' (V, 1845–6), and therefore the poet, too, entrusts his poem to Christ's hands. But the higher reformulation of the human/divine, natural/spiritual dichotomy, which is presaged by Troilus' ascent to the eighth sphere, does not eliminate the narrator's problem of how to fuse approval and condemnation of Troilus' and Criseyde's love within the framework of a fictional story.[41] It is true that the narrator's function has been to point out all the possible mechanisms in such a complex love: tragic and comic aspects of it are stressed in turn. But then the rupture between the pagan and the Christian world is made apparent at the end of Book V in the two stanzas that address the book itself, the tangible product of *his* writing, which the poet is afraid might not be understood. Only *after* mention has been made of the book that circumscribes the human story of Troilus and Criseyde – and thus *outside* the pagan context – can Troilus' death and his ascent to the place allotted by Mercury take place, thanks to Christ's mercy, 'Uncircumscript, and al maist circumscrive' (V, 1865).

The strength of the ending of *Troilus* lies therefore in leaving the conclusion of the work open once again, not because of an interruption as in the *House of Fame*, but by means of the re-presentation in synthesis of the problems connected with Chaucer's role as poet and specifically as a Christian poet. All the cards have been laid on the table: the pagan past (the story passed down), the present (Chaucer's book narrating the story) and the eschatological future (which *may* allow a solution to Troilus' story). The latter, which is the future in relation to the 'histori-

41 For a significant contribution to the meaning of the ending of the *Troilus*, see Wetherbee, *Chaucer and the Poets*, pp. 224–43, who points out Chaucer's new awareness of the role and capacities of poetry and of *his* poem. The departure from Boccaccio shown at the end of *Troilus* is discussed by J. Dean, 'Chaucer's *Troilus*, Boccaccio's *Filostrato*, and the Poetics of Closure', *Philological Quarterly* 64 (1985) 175–84. On Dante's influence, see B. Wheeler, 'Dante, Chaucer, and the Ending of *Troilus and Criseyde*', *Philological Quarterly* 61 (1982) 105–23, and E. D. Kirk, '"Paradis Stood Formed in Hire Yen": Courtly Love and Chaucer's Re-Vision of Dante', in M. J. Carruthers and E. D. Kirk, eds., *Acts of Interpretation. The Text in Its Context. 700–1600* (Norman, 1982), pp. 257–77, where Troilus' love is seen as the only possible response left to Chaucer in a world so different from Dante's.

cal' dimension of Troilus, is the true present for Christian Chaucer and for his audience. But Chaucer the poet can never overcome the obstacle of Troilus' paganism: Christ alone, within the linear a-temporality of the universe, can embrace the pagan past.

CHAPTER TWO

'Atwixen two so hang I in balaunce': Lydgate and the *Temple of Glas*

It is December. The poet cannot sleep and dreams of a 'temple of glas'. When he enters it, he sees many lovers complaining to Venus and notices that the walls are painted with images of sorrowful lovers. Some of the ladies in the temple complain about their forced marriages and among them one is singled out for her excellent beauty. The lady is bound to somebody she does not love, and Venus answers her complaint vaguely. Then the knight is introduced and his speech is in the courtly language tradition. Venus promises her help and suggests he should open his heart to the lady. The knight utters his complaint to the lady, and she replies with words of hope for the future. Venus unites the two lovers with a kind of marriage bond. After a 'ballade' dedicated to the goddess, the poem ends with the poet's awakening and his promise to write a 'litil tretise' (1380) in praise of women. A short envoy follows.

The reader approaching Lydgate's text immediately runs into a series of difficulties. Almost everything that can be said seems to have been said about the poem, from its debt to Chaucer's *House of Fame* and *Parliament of Fowls* to its formal and thematic innovations. For Schirmer 'Lydgate is imitative in his choice of subject-matter and mode of expression and remote from life in his archaic book-knowledge and predilection for rhetoric',[1] whereas for Renoir 'Lydgate's preoccupation with the individual human being allows him to express what earlier poets of courtly love have failed even to suspect'.[2] According to Spearing, Lydgate's worst fault lies in his being an imitator of Chaucer and not writing like

1 W. F. Schirmer, *John Lydgate. A Study in the Culture of the XVth Century*, translated A. E. Keep (Westport, Conn., 1961), p. 38.

2 A. Renoir, *The Poetry of John Lydgate* (London, 1967), p. 93. Renoir had already pointed out Lydgate's understanding of human suffering in his article, 'Attitudes Toward Women in Lydgate's Poetry', *English Studies* 42 (1961) 1–14, especially pp. 12–13.

him: the poem is a fabric of incongruities whose *significaunce* escapes the reader.[3] In his excellent edition of the *Poems* J. Norton-Smith identifies the philosophical schema enunciated in *De Consolatione Philosophiae* IV, pr. 2 as the source of the dominant allegory in the *Temple*: this schema affirms that all things can be known and defined in terms of their opposites.[4] Derek Pearsall, even though he stresses that the originality of the poem consists in the fact that 'it takes as its "story" a literal human situation',[5] concludes his analysis by admitting that Lydgate manages 'to suggest the sameness of everything'.[6]

After all that has been said there would not seem to be any room left for further approaches to the poem. Yet a close reading of the text will allow us to clarify certain problems that still remain about the ultimate meaning of the *Temple of Glas*. That it is an imitation of various of Chaucer's poems is true, but it is also true that it abandons the Chaucerian model in the importance given to the lady and in a 'new' use of a standardized imagery. Its debt to Chaucer and the classics, to Boethius and the *Roman de la Rose*, is undeniable,[7] but Lydgate's treatment of this material, on more careful examination, proves to be very interesting. This provides the justification for a textual analysis whose starting-point is the linguistic definition of most of the commonplaces concerning the lady. This will lead on to a (re)definition of the role of the individual and of that special individual, the poet, in his relation to past and present.

The syntagma of the poem's title is characteristic: the association of *temple* and *glas* is in the nature of an oxymoron, and it is by means of this that Lydgate hints at a series of oppositions inherited from Boethius through Chaucer. This does not imply that I am denying the influence of the *House of Fame* – the image of the temple makes it plain enough – nor am I denying the debt to *Troilus*. What I want to point out is the feeling of instability, of uncertainty that exists in the poem along with the theme of constancy in love and with the brightness and luminosity evoked by a wealth of similes. The temple, an enclosed space used for

3 A. C. Spearing, *Medieval Dream-Poetry* (Cambridge, 1976), pp. 171–6.

4 J. Norton-Smith, ed., *John Lydgate: Poems* (Oxford, 1966), p. 177; all quotations of the *Temple of Glas* are from this edition.

5 D. Pearsall, *John Lydgate* (London, 1970), p. 107.

6 Pearsall, *J. Lydgate*, p. 115. See also by the same author, 'The English Chaucerians', in *Chaucer and Chaucerians*, ed. D. S. Brewer (London, 1966), pp. 201–39.

7 For the influence of Boethius, of the *Roman de la Rose* and of Chaucer on the *Temple of Glas* see Pearsall, *J. Lydgate*, pp. 104–15, and Norton-Smith, *J. Lydgate*, pp. 176–91.

contemplation ('a contemplatione templum'),[8] represents, with its perfect circular structure, solidity, certainty. At the beginning, however, this function of meditation is denied, because the dreamer is prevented from entering the temple by the material it is built of, sunlight-reflecting glass.

The darkness of the December night (on earth) has its counterpart in the darkness of the clouds (in the dream) that allow the dreamer to enter the temple 'ful fer in wildirnes' (17), without being blinded. The glass that the temple is made of has two precise connotations: luminosity, accentuated by the sunlight reflected by it, and the capacity for metaphorical – if not physical – disintegration, in the sense that its potential excess of power to reflect precludes the dreamer's entrance.

Once inside the temple, the dreamer sees, painted on the walls, pictures of famous lovers appealing to Venus. The divinity to whom the *Temple of Glas* is dedicated is therefore Venus, and it is her presence that emphasizes the ambiguity of the temple. The goddess is a symbol of love, of fertility and consequently of the continuity of life. However, because of her iconographic association with the mirror (which by the fifteenth century was made of glass), she is also a symbol of vanity, instability, and transitoriness.[9]

That love may also beguile and cause pain is made manifest by the first classical example of an unhappy lover, Dido, deceived by Aeneas' 'hestis' and 'oþis sworne' (59). Inside the temple the walls therefore act as mirrors in the sense that the lady, as we shall see, is mirrored by, and identified through the classical stories of lovers. After a long description Lydgate turns to other lovers – real, not painted ones. These complain of all the possible distresses to which falling in love is subject: *Ielousie, absence, Daunger, Disdain* and various constraints. In this way the poet brings the reader's attention back to love's still vital problems and builds up to the climax – the appearance of the poem's central character, the lady. Her surpassing beauty is described by what would seem to be every available commonplace drawn from the inanimate as well as the animate world, and extending even to comparison with Phoebus (272).

That the woman, like the temple and its interior, should be thought of as a mirror is foreshadowed by the vision the dreamer has: 'Beside Pallas wiþ hir cristal sheld' (248), 'knelid a ladi in my siȝt' (250), –

8 Isidore, *Etymologiae* XV, iv, 7.

9 On the association between Venus and the mirror see H. Schwarz, 'The Mirror in Art', *The Art Quarterly* 15 (1952) 97–118, pp. 106–9 and M. Twycross, *The Medieval Anadyomene* (Oxford, 1972), pp. 82–8.

Lydgate is referring, of course, to the mythological episode in which Pallas' shield has already acted as a mirror to allow Perseus to kill Medusa. Here 'Lich Phebus bemys shynyng in his spere' (272), because of the lady's noble presence, 'The tempil was enlumynd environ' (283). Outside the temple the light given by Phoebus, the Sun, illuminates the surrounding space, while inside it is the lady who acts as a reflecting element. She gives back light in the same way as a transparent element does: she allows her inner and also her outer qualities to be perceived as norms of behaviour corresponding to the canons of courtly ethic and Christian moral virtues, these latter destined to be a source of suffering.[10]

The passive/active dichotomy latent in the mirror metaphor completely characterizes the woman.[11] On the one hand she represents a 'meruaile' (267), a creature exceptional among Nature's works and described by the poet in terms of the traditional commonplaces. She is 'So aungellike, so goodli on to se' (269) and 'So replenysshid of beaute and of grace, / So wel ennuyd bi Nature and depeint' (274–5). On the other hand the lady is 'wel', 'rote', 'exemplarie' and a 'mirrour' 'Of secrenes, of trouth, of faythfulnes, / And to al oþer ladi and maistres, / To sue vertu, whoso list to lere' (295–7); that is, she stands as an example for other women. The lady, whose light shines forth in the temple, is defined both by specifically courtly virtues ('bounte', 'gentilles', 'curtesie', 'daliaunce') and by more generically Christian virtues ('trouth', 'faythfulnes'). The motto 'De Mieulx En Mieulx' at the end of the description of the lady is itself a synthesis of all the qualities the woman so admirably possesses.

The other, less fortunate aspect of the lady, who has shortly before appeared in the full authority of her perfection, is revealed by the words of her 'litel bil' (317): just as the painted lovers and just as the lovers wandering in the temple do, this lady suffers and grieves. There are two reasons for this: the marriage bond that prevents her from loving truly, and the impossibility of her true love ever being fulfilled.

When, therefore, she proclaims

> Atwixen two so hang I in balaunce, (348)

10 See C. S. Lewis, *The Allegory of Love* (Oxford, 1936), pp. 239–43, where he stresses Lydgate's 'modern' conception of love as well as his ambiguous attitude towards marriage and true love.

11 On the ambivalence of the mirror metaphor, see F. Goldin, *The Mirror of Narcissus in the Courtly Love Lyric* (Ithaca, N.Y., 1967), pp. 4–15.

we begin to understand how Lydgate is pointing out the division within the woman herself, completely reversing everything the dreamer/narrator has said about her. How can the lady be a mirror in the sense of an example of virtues like faith and constancy if she herself represents division, the loss of equipoise, – 'Mi þouȝt goþe forþe, mi bodi is behind' (346)? Is it perhaps precisely because of this 'human nature' of hers that she can be presented as a truer example, in that she approximates reality? If so, then not all of Lydgate's *amplificatio* can be seen as a gross overworking of his material. He has in fact followed the Boethian precept[12] and succeeded in uniting two opposing images of woman which, according to the canons of courtly poetry, were very different and mutually exclusive.

The description and the petition of the lover that follow belong to courtly tradition with all the classical paraphernalia of Cupid and his arrow, the beloved's absolute and unconditional devotion, the negative intervention of personifications such as 'Drede', 'Daunger' and 'Dispeire' opposed by positive 'Hope'. Yet this poem also requires that love be described in new and more complex terms than the traditional ones.

Love for Lydgate is not to be looked at only from the point of view of the man appealing to a woman made of ice, but from the woman's point of view as well. She is suffering because she would like to be free to choose to love to the full – with body and soul. This central point is emphasized by the lady, since she says at line 336: 'Freli to chese þere lak I liberte', and again at line 353: 'To my desire contrarie is my mede'. Thus the lady not only illuminates the temple with her virtues, but she also concentrates and reflects the characteristics of grief and woe that the other women embody. The women who grieve inside the temple are obliged, like her, to 'shew þe contrarie outward of her hert' (206) and are 'Wiþoute fredom of eleccioun' (211).

Then what is Lydgate aiming at in the juxtaposition of images reflected in and by the lady? It is not easy to find an answer, and the attempt is complicated by the obsessive repetition of the mirror metaphor, a frequent one in Lydgate's poetry.[13] The 'human' nature of the lady's sentiments is at once put into correct perspective by what Venus says. To console the lady she attributes the cause of her sufferings to Saturn; she recalls examples of joy following on adversity (she cites

12 Boethius, *De Consolatione Philosophiae* IV, pr. 2.

13 See the examples from Lydgate's works quoted in H. Grabes, *The Mutable Glass* (Cambridge, 1982), pp. 378–9.

'Grisilde', 'Penalope' and 'Dorigene' as cases in point) and thus prophesies a general but vague solution to the woman's woes.

The subsequent invocation of the lover to Venus again shows us the woman's function as mirror of inner and outer qualities: this occurs just half way through the poem, in stanzas 7 and 8, which offer, in a mirror form, a summa of the lady's characteristics:

7

'For in myn hert enprintid is so sore
Hir shap, hir fourme, and al hir semelines,
Hir port, hir chere, hir goodnes more and more,
Hir womanhede and eke hir gentilnes,
Hir trouth, hir faiþ and [eke] hir kynd[e]nes,
With al vertues, iche set in his degre:
There is no lak, saue onli of pite.

8

'Hir sad demening, of wil not variable,
Of looke benynge and roote of al plesaunce,
And exemplaire to al þat wil be stable,
Discrete, prudent, of wisdom suffisaunce,
Mirrour of wit, ground of gouernaunce,
A world of beaute compassid in hir face,
Whose persant loke doþ þuruȝ myn hert[e] race. (743–56)

There is a correspondence between the first line of stanza 7 (743), 'For in myn hert enprintid is so sore' (passive), and the cause of the suffering specified in line 756, 'Whose persant loke doþ þuruȝ myn hert[e] race'. 'Persant', here attributed to the lady's look, recalls the 'persing' of line 25 attributed to the too dazzling sunlight. The outer qualities relative to physical appearance detailed in stanza 7 are matched in stanza 8 by the listing of inner virtues. The poet repeats previously used terms such as 'roote', 'exemplaire', 'mirrour', 'ground', from line 751 down to line 755, 'A world of beaute compassid in hir face', with its Neoplatonic conception of the woman's face as a microcosm of beauty.[14] After presenting the lady as an example of inner and outer beauty beyond compare, the lover must once more make use of classical stereo-

[14] See J. Frappier, 'Variations sur le thème du miroir, de Bernard de Ventadour à Maurice Scève', *Cahiers de l'Association Internationale des Études Françaises* 11 (1959) 134–58, especially pp. 151–2, and E. Köhler, 'Narcisse, la fontaine d'Amour et Guillaume de Lorris', *Journal des Savants* (Avril – Juin 1963) 86–103.

types of faithfulness to explain to omniscient Venus the steadfastness and fidelity of his love. In this he echoes the dreamer's presentation of the stories painted on the walls at the beginning of the dream.

At this point it is necessary to examine the mirror structure of the text. Like all dream-vision poems, the *Temple of Glas* offers us a narrator who is also the dreamer of the dream recounted. Often he breaks into the story, interrupting the continuity of the dream with observations on writing, or on the difficulty of remembering and communicating. The mirror construction can be noted on two separate planes: the dream story is the inner plane and the framework the outer one,[15] and the temple serves to contain them both.

The mirror nature of the subject-matter, that is, of the inner plane represented by the story, is very complex. The theme is that of unhappy love, and to this belong the lady's love-story, the love-stories of the grieving women and those of the painted pictures. From the characteristics attributed to her, the lady could be defined as a mirror. She contains all the inner and outer qualities of the ideal woman: she is a kind of *speculum*, a compilation of morals and manners. Yet, since she epitomizes all these aspects, the lady also embodies the elements of grief and unhappiness present in the two series of lovers: she is an unhappy lover because she is bound against her will, even though she is root, source and mirror of physical and spiritual beauty.

The seven stanzas of the lady's invocation at first seem antithetic to the dreamer's and the man's descriptions. In their descriptions she appears as an abstract example of virtue, while in the invocation she is presented concretely in her historical setting, which is dramatically present in the clear reference to a social tie – which may be marriage. The concept of constraint is recalled by terms such as 'The bodi knyt' (338), 'to be knit vndir subieccion' (344), 'ilaced in a chaine' (355), which culminate in 'closid is my wounde' (362), that is, in the intimate acceptance of suffering.

The rhetorical taste for antitheses, which derives from Boethius,[16] acquires dramatic importance in the continual oppositions that recur in

15 On the dream frame of the *Temple of Glas* see the interesting essay by J. M. Davidoff, 'The Audience Illuminated, or New Light Shed on the Dream Frame of Lydgate's *Temple of Glas*', *Studies in the Age of Chaucer* 5 (1983) 103–25, in which the focus is on the complex opposition between 'light' and the lack of it and on the audience's responses to Lydgate's subtle rhetorical devices. On the significance of the framing fiction in fifteenth century narrative, see, by the same author, *Beginning Well. Framing Fictions in Late Middle English Poetry* (Rutherford, 1988).

16 Cf. note 4.

the woman's invocation, oppositions involving body and spirit (mind, thought, recollection), will (desire) and reality (everyday concerns), all of them summarized in the impressive two-line chiastic structure:

> Mi þouȝt goþe forþe, mi bodi is behind,
> For I am here and yonde my remembraunce. (346–7)

On one hand, there is the hard reality of the body and the self forced into remaining still, on the other the great freedom of recollection and thought marked by the two adverbs 'forþe' and 'yonde'. Lack of freedom is therefore connected with the body and with being part of society: the sole freedom is inner freedom. The chances of escape are limited to thought and recollection: they are almost the fruit of fantasy. The way is open to 'boþ witte and mynde' (345) to travel far and wide, but the dramatic problem of the limits imposed by society is synthesized in the line 'Freli to chese þere lak I liberte' (336).

According to some modern theorists, the mirror metaphor for these body/thought, 'wille'/'dede' antitheses may serve as a revealing element of the double conflict within and without the individual, between the inner and outer self and, by means of language, between the inner self and the external elements that modify the outer self.[17]

It is Venus with all her attributes of luminosity, transparency, reflection, who acts as the mirror that reveals the lady. Venus is characterized by marks such as 'discerne' (326), 'consider' (367), 'se' (367), and though she replies, she gives a vague answer to the lady's request, in effect confirming the *status quo* of grief and pain. Venus here thus represents instinctual love, the stage the lady has gone beyond, that of the pleasurable recognition of the self.[18] This has been replaced by the tension that comes from the acceptance of the division between self-fulfilment on the one hand, and social constraints on the other, between, in ideal terms, the freedom to choose, and, in real terms, the hindrances deriving from society. The tie (which we can assume to be marriage)

[17] See J. Lacan, 'Le Stade du miroir comme formateur de la fonction du "je" ', in *Écrits I* (Paris, 1966) pp. 89–97, where the 'mirror stage' in the psychological development of the infant is seen as marking a transformation that leads to an awareness of the influence of social and cultural structures upon the self: 'Ce moment où s'achève le stade du miroir inaugure, par l'identification à l'*imago* du semblable . . . la dialectique qui dès lors lie le *je* à des situations socialement élaborées' (p. 95).

[18] Cf. Lacan, 'Le Stade', p. 90.

imposed from without involves a gradual recognition that the inner split or division itself has become internalized.[19]

For the natural instincts totality has been fractured by rules imposed from the outside – 'Thogh we be on, þe dede most varie' (341): it is on this basis that Lydgate depicts a condition of static tension, of suspension between the two poles of the division – 'Atwixen two so hang I in balaunce' (348), that is, between the body bound to reality, and the thought free to express the inner self. The consequence of this is a final 'normalization', that is, an acceptance of discord and hence of society's power to alienate. 'Of wille and dede ilaced in a chaine' (355) and 'That hatter brenne þat closid is my wounde' (362) is the price that must be paid to the social role of the lady, in that the wound, that is, the division, is perforce closed by acceptance.

Recomposition, the internalization following on it, and the oppositions that are thus reconciled are further pointed out by the lady's answer to Venus (461–502). In fact, the goddess has done no more than stress the lover's service and homage to the lady, vaguely promising happiness as a just reward for the lady's suffering. But the problem does not lie in this.

The lady's dilemma lay in making the choice not between body and spirit, but between on the one hand the desire to satisfy her sensual instincts and on the other the behaviour, the action ('dede') that causes her to conform to the rules of the social and religious contract:[20] this is the irreconcilable choice she is faced with.

The lady changes register completely when she answers Venus: she declares that she has made peace with herself and has banished all grief since the goddess has guaranteed the constancy of the lover's 'service', 'That he ne shal varie' (485). But was this what she desired? In her first invocation she had spoken only of the impossibility of (physically) returning his true love, because of the rules made and applied both by courtly culture and by Christian doctrine and society: now in her reply to the goddess she removes the inner division and declares herself reconciled to outer service from the lover.

In the man's subsequent complaint (567–693) we find the same terms as in the lady's invocation, but their meaning is often different. He too is 'bound þat whilom was so fre / And went at laarge at myn eleccioun'

19 Lacan, 'Le Stade', p. 99.

20 On marriage as an economic business in the late Middle Ages, see S. Medcalf, ed., *The Later Middle Ages* (London, 1981), pp. 231–43.

(568–9), he too is 'vnder subieccioun' (570) and joined to the God of love 'within his fire cheyne' (574), but his ties, his loss of freedom, his subjection to the lady and to the language with which all the elements are described are all part of a particular world which, though it belongs to the past by now, is still credible. The lover's references to the God of love, to the vanity of trying to flee him by engaging battle – where the sole victor is the woman – to the struggle between Hope and Drede (typical personifications of courtly poetry), derive from a tradition of poetry still held in high esteem.[21]

Stanzas 7 and 8 – which I referred to earlier – with their specular and circular form stressing the lady's perfection – repeat the poem's rhetoric, but now on a different plane from what the woman's speech has led us to expect; it is a repetition that recalls the healing of the inner fracture by virtue of the conventional sentiment expressed in the lady's last words (1057–1102). The lover's request (836–40) that Cupid light a spark in her heart is again a step backwards, given that the lady has never made any question of her love.

Why then does the poet insist on proceeding with a stop/go, backwards/forwards motion? Venus does her part in stressing the apparent similarity in the lady's and the man's state by urging both of them to persevere in their honest behaviour, because joy will follow grief. Venus advises the lover to make his love and his desire to serve her known to the lady, because nothing can be attained without words: the wound that is not shown to the doctor cannot be treated (916–17). Language then, the language of words, may encompass perfection and unhappiness, and thus the fracture – or indeed the various fractures – will be healed, even though the healing will be painful.

On the one hand we have a man anxious to display his devotion and submission to his idealized beloved, to him the emblem of beauty and perfection; on the other we have a woman who is well aware of her inner dichotomy between self and society: once the lady, the perfect embodiment of the courtly lady, has gone beyond the first phase of recognizing personal sensual love she behaves according to the rules of religion and society which she also perfectly embodies:

> For so demeyned she was in honeste
> That vnavised noþing hir astert:
> So mych of reson was compast in hir hert. (1051–3)

[21] On the popularity of dream poetry in this period, see Schirmer, *J. Lydgate*, pp. 36–7.

It is rationality that now dominates the lady's heart, and the Venus she addresses has come correspondingly to stand for Divinity, that is, for the orthodoxy that must guarantee love's being lived ideally until such time as the lady's 'legal' status changes and allows fulfilment to her love. The bond with which Venus unites the two lovers is indeed a chain 'of stele' (1120) and the virtue she urges is constancy in their ideal love.

Venus too, who has iconographic and conceptual links with the mirror,[22] undergoes variations in meaning, which are often present side by side. And it is precisely as a mirror that Venus acts, in the sense that she allows the lady to glimpse the dual relationship between herself and the other, between the inner self and the outer, in a play of reflections that is stressed by the goddess' prerogatives of luminosity inside the temple of glass (itself a mirror). Just as the mirror reveals the oppositions within the woman's soul ('herte'), and then gives rise to detailed linguistic considerations on the oppositions, so too Venus is transformed on the *symbolic* plane and develops into the force which decides and orders that the lady's instinctual drives be reabsorbed into the social ambit.[23]

As Lydgate presents her, Venus becomes a substitute for both God and the Establishment, in that she concentrates in herself and synthesizes the crystallizations of such social qualities as constancy, faithfulness, chastity, and all the stereotypes of Lydgate's society.[24] The 'golden cheyne' of line 1106 with which Venus seals the ideal union between the two is not much different from the tie that unites the woman to the 'þing þat I nold' (335): in both cases psychological and material union is impossible, in that the lady must await a change in her condition, before achieving her happiness. It is impossible for her to have the 'other' (the lover) merely because she does not want the 'other' (the husband) she already has.

Now, the process of socialization in an individual – the beginning of a relationship with the other – is always a moment, or rather a series of moments, of progressive tension within and/or without the individual himself. In this context Venus cannot do other than urge on the lover

22 See note 9.

23 On the role of language in the 'mirror stage', see G. Rosolato, 'Le narcissisme', *Nouvelle Revue de Psychanalyse* 13 (1976) 7–36; see also A. Lemaire, *Jacques Lacan* (Bruxelles, 1977), ch. II: 'Philosophie du langage chez Jacques Lacan', pp. 99–118, especially pp. 102–3.

24 See Lemaire, *J. Lacan*, p. 109 and p. 112: 'La relation entre les hommes va se médiatiser par le discours ou, plus précisément, par les concepts qu'il engendre. Et dans le domaine du symbolisme social, le troisième terme médiateur entre les vivants sera l'Ancétre, la Mort, le Dieu, la Cause sacrée, l'Institution, l'idéologie, etc.'.

the practice of virtue and the horror of vice, and on the lady constancy, humility and faithfulness according to the conventional rules of society. The final outlet of the tension is another bond never to be broken on pain of the gods' vengeance, an ideal bond between the two lovers that the goddess only offers as a prospect in the dream temple. The gods of the alliance, Saturn, Jove, Mars and Cupid, who stands for Venus herself here, may be considered in their role as planets connected with the humours (melancholy: Saturn; blood: Jove; choler: Mars; phlegm: Moon or Venus), the elements of which all human beings are constituted.[25] The gods' vengeance on the faithless lover would therefore consist in an alteration in the lover's humours resulting from the upheaval in the influence of the planets that they are related to.

Lydgate's insistence on the theory of opposites derived from Boethius shows his practice of imitating, but it also stresses the concept of division, of fracture, which is the basis of all forms of knowledge. Just as a knowledge of white is impossible without the notion of black, and happiness cannot be appreciated by those who have not experienced grief, so one cannot be a conscious interpreter of ways of thought and behaviour – in short, of one's culture – without paying the price in tension, and more than this, in sacrifice of one's own immediate desire. In the end, as Venus has promised, the lady will achieve a new and complete happiness, but she must first experience the fracture of pain (within) and the rules of society (without). Even in the final ballad of joy for the ideal union that has been contracted, Venus is thanked for having allowed the man to serve the lady 'withoute synne' (1346), not contravening, that is, any moral law – a point that was vital for a monk like Lydgate.

But we would be mistaken if we thought that at the end of the dream happiness reigns – even on an ideal plane. This interpretation is denied by the continual insistence on the *necessity* of grief, which is repeated in the dream and outside the dream (the heart of the dreamer/poet himself is full of 'gret þouȝt and wo' – 1370), and by the fact that happiness is once again delayed. Furthermore, the words and actions of the goddess have only served to rearrange the order of priorities. In her first invocation the lady asked for the chance to be united forever with her lover, to possess the object of her desire: in this her request differs from the man's,

[25] See R. Klibansky, E. Panofsky, F. Saxl, *Saturn and Melancholy* (London, 1964), part II, ch. 1.

a lover torn between Hope and Drede, still linguistically tied to courtly stereotypes. In Venus the inner conflict of the woman is transformed into a conflict with social institutions, and this brings about a solution to the conflict, in that the very terms of the tension are disregarded.

At this point we need to look more closely at the specular nature of the framework of the story, at what holds the dream-vision together, in an attempt to grasp that 'significaunce' that still escapes us in the poem. As Derek Pearsall has pointed out, the structure of the *Temple* is rather complex and sophisticated with its division into groups of stanzas for the lyrical parts and the narrative introduction, and couplets joining the various parts.[26] This formal pattern, which derives from but modifies Chaucer,[27] reveals a series of parallels of similar and dissimilar elements which is worth noting: it is at the points where the structure is less tightly knit that the poet's tension in presenting a 'difficult' love story comes to the surface.

The real or imaginary cause of the dream lies in a great sorrow for an impossible love – or one possible only on certain conditions. The aim of the poem which narrates the dream is to send a message to a woman whom the poet desires but is not *permitted* to love (whether he identifies with the lover/dreamer is of no importance). That the woman the poem is destined for is 'my ladi' of line 1392 and the lady of the dream herself is suggested by the poem's context, which is characterized by a considerable degree of deliberate ambiguity.

In the *Temple of Glas* Lydgate uses the two *personae*, Venus and the dreamer/poet, to recount two stories: on the one hand, Venus constructs the love story between the lady and the man, on the other, the dreamer/poet recounts the story 'constructed' by Venus. In the waking episodes stress is laid on the poet who cannot sleep, who then dreams, and who at the end of the dream promises to write a treatise in honour of women: in the dream itself, however, it is the woman who is both subject and object of the 'desire' that should lead to the enjoyment of love.

In both situations of double identity (Venus and the poet as characters and narrators) there are elements of reticence and tension that allude to the hidden meaning of the poem. The goddess, as Derek Pearsall says,[28] acts as a mouthpiece, in that she allows the connection

26 Pearsall, *J. Lydgate*, p. 106.
27 *Ibidem*.
28 Pearsall, *J. Lydgate*, p. 107.

between the two lovers and is herself the cause of their love: she is, however, reticent about the events leading up to the present situation. Venus progressively suppresses her identity as a mythological goddess (even though she makes frequent references to her unfortunate father Saturn and her son Cupid) and increasingly speaks in terms of a Christian priest ratifying a bond of an almost matrimonial nature between a couple. Venus as the inspirer of desire is clearly prior to the lady's invocation, but the episode of the woman's falling in love is scarcely touched on, and the point at which Cupid actually hits the man with his arrow is also neglected.

Lydgate's emphasis on the woman and her *desire* to possess another man, a different one from the one she has, is a way of drawing tighter the bonds that hold a woman to the rules of a man-centred and man-oriented society, in which the consciousness of sin is associated with woman more than man.[29] The woman is a mirror of perfection in the dreamer/poet's description, and the motto 'De Mieulx En Mieulx' emphasizes the idea of perfection as progression. The motto itself ties the description of the lady's excellence to the invocation to Venus – an ambiguous goddess of love who can decide the fate of unhappy lovers; indeed, as the dreamer reminds us, the lady has a great desire: 'Forto compleyne' (316). Furthermore, because of her complaint, the lady is associated in the temple with the women painted on the walls, the multifarious list of whom is headed by Dido, the queen betrayed by Aeneas, the son of Venus, who herself appears shortly after with Adonis. In Chaucer's *House of Fame* Venus and Dido are two complementary aspects of love, and of tragic love at that.[30]

Why does Lydgate choose to make the connection between the two stories – the 'fabula' consisting of the imaginary episodes belonging to mythological tradition which had come down to him from the pens of various authors, and *his* 'fabula' of the lady and the man's love? The easiest answer might be that Lydgate found everything ready and to hand in Chaucer, but that would be a refusal to acknowledge the work of the medieval poet whose poetic art – as Dorothy Everett observes with regard to Chaucer – does not lie in creating something new, but rather in selecting, uniting and presenting the already known in new and varied ways.[31] And when an author selects, he makes a choice.

29 See Medcalf, *The Later Middle Ages*, pp. 239–41.
30 See P. Boitani, *Chaucer and the Imaginary World of Fame* (Cambridge, 1984), p. 182.
31 D. Everett, *Essays on Middle English Literature*, ed. P. Kean (Oxford, 1955), p. 107.

In so well-ordered a structure as the *Temple*, what is not said alludes continually to something that cannot be said. There is ambiguity in the two dual roles, dreamer/narrator and Venus/narrator, where the subjects of the two 'fabulae' are exchanged: Venus narrates, or rather invents, the 'fabula' of the lady and her lover, and the poet narrates the 'fabula' of the mythological stories on the temple walls, thus further complicating the reading of the poem. At the beginning the suffering of the dreamer in his room is at once evident, without, however, our being explicitly told the cause of it. Equally evident is the suffering of the dreamer inside his dream, because he does not succeed in entering the temple except after great effort, and by a 'wiket' (39) rather than the main door. And the temple refers at the same time to both poetry and love – the poetry of the classical Chaucerian tradition from which the stories are taken, but also the poetry of the dreamer/poet who places *his* love-story, the last in the line of tradition, in the temple.

Love is always threatened with suffering, whether in famous lovers or in the lady and the man, because deep down there is a potential situation for betrayal, for adultery, whether this is actually committed or not. The lexical indications of the guilty state of the two lovers are frequent, even though they are only indirect (for example, when Venus promises that the man will love his lady 'Wiþoute spot of eny doubelnes' – 441 and 't'eschwe euere synne and vice' – 450, and so on), and the guilty situation concerning the poet is pointed out just as frequently. At the beginning of the second part the dreamer/poet appears much surer of himself than in the first, so much so that he steps aside from the crowd gathered in the temple and walks about 'þe estres' (549) by himself until he meets the man. Among other things the lover complains that:

> 'For lak of spech I can sey nov nomore:
> I haue mater but I can not plein:
> Mi wit is dulle to telle al my sore. (820–2)

After Venus answers, urging the lover to make his love known to the lady with the proper words, there comes one of the most interesting parts of the poem, where the poet questions himself on his nature as poet and on writing poetry. The narrative from line 932 to line 969 contains the parallel descriptions of the man's and the poet's sufferings. Both suffer, deep down, for love (and the dreamer/poet perhaps identifies with the lover); as concerns the story, however, the problem lies in communicating this suffering. The lover is overcome by fear: 'To put him forþe forto tel his peyne / Vnto his ladi, oþer to compleyne' (942–3) and the poet is defeated by compassion: 'That, wel vnneþe þouȝ with myself I striue, / I want connyng his peynes to discryue' (950–1).

Communication is always difficult and painful whether on the lover's or the poet's part. The cause of this difficulty is easy to determine at a first, superficial reading. The lover, according to the canons of love poetry, is afraid of laying himself open to rebuff and the poet, bound by the *exordium* convention, underestimates his own ability, as he also does, in almost the same words, in *A Complaynt of a Loveres Lyfe*.[32] If we bear in mind, however, the theme of desire leading perforce, in the two lovers' situation, to adultery, the man's reticence is to be placed alongside the pauses and the silence that surround the falling-in-love phase for both the lady and himself. The final cause of their falling in love is Venus, goddess of eros.

There remains the reticence of the poet to be explained. It is symptomatic that he cannot appeal to the Muses, the divinities that provide inspiration 'in maters þat þe[m] delite also' (955), but only to Tisiphone and her sisters, the Furies, divinities of torment and suffering. This invocation too is a topos: it is to be found in the fourth book of Chaucer's *Troilus*[33] and is also used by Lydgate in the *Fall of Princes*,[34] the Furies here being associated with the Fates. And of course the association Fates/Furies is present also in the *Roman de la Rose* where Genius, in his speech, puts the readers on their guard against straying from the straight and narrow paths trod by their forebears: 'Se ne fust leur chevalerie, / Vous ne fussiez pas ore en vie' (If it weren't for their chivalry,

32 *A Complaynt of a Loveres Lyfe* in Norton-Smith, *J. Lydgate*:

> But who shal helpe me now to compleyn?
> Or who shal now my stile guy or lede?
> O Nyobe, let now thi teres reyn
> Into my pen; and eke helpe in this nede,
> Thou woful Myrre that felist my[n] hert blede
> Of pitous wo, eke my[n] honde quake
> When that I write for this mannys sake. (176–82)

33 *Troilus and Criseyde* Book IV, ll. 22–8.

34 'An Exclamatioun of the Deth of Alcibiades' (*Fall of Princes*, III) in Norton-Smith, *J. Lydgate*:

> O out on Styx and out on Attropos,
> That han of malis slayn so good a kniht.
> Out on you thre that kepe yoursilff so clos,
> Douhtres icallid of the dirke niht.
> And thou Letum, that quenchest eke the liht
> Of Alcibiades, merour and lanterne
> To speke in knihthod how men hem shold gouerne. (3662–8)

you would not be alive now; 19787–8). The Furies are presented as 'Les treis ribaudes felonesses, / Des felonies vencherresses' (The three cruel pursurers, the avengers of crimes; 19833–4) and connected in Genius' speech with the traitors to the good knightly traditions.[35]

Moreover, this relationship of the Furies with man's overweening pride appears in the *Roman* only shortly before Jean de Meun's criticism of Guillaume de Lorris, and Lydgate must have been aware of this. For this reason the invocation to the Furies (addressed in the 'Exclamacioun' 3664 as 'on you thre that kepe yoursilff so clos' – that is, presented in silence) should not simply be taken at the surface level of the poem. Although the situation of the two lovers here in the *Temple* should find a happy solution, may it not be that Lydgate introduces the Furies because he wants to stress again the consciousness of sin that remains in spite of everything? The sinning is twofold: the lovers' sin *in spite of* Venus' intervention (and *because of* Venus' having aroused their passion) and the poet's sin of having, like Jean de Meun's barons and Niobe in the *Complaynt*, allowed himself to be governed by pride.

The poet's sin is twofold. He sins because, monk though he is, he presents a love triangle of dubious morality.[36] He also sins against classical and medieval traditions (against the *auctores* such as Virgil, Chaucer, etc.) because his way of conceiving writing is different:

> I can no ferþer but to Thesiphone
> And to hir sustren forto help[e] me
> That bene goddesses of turment and of peyne.
> Nou lete ȝoure teris into myn inke reyne,
> With woful woordis my pauper forto blot,
> This woful mater to peint[e] not but spotte. (958–63)

In this passage it would seem that Lydgate is making use of the 'ut pictura poesis' commonplace in order to re-evaluate it.[37] The walls of the temple shaped into a circle, the perfect geometrical form, are all painted

35 All quotations are from E. Langlois, ed., *Le Roman de la Rose* (Paris, 1914–24), 5 vols, vol. 5, transl. C. Dahlberg (Hanover and London, 1986).

36 See A. D. Scaglione, *Nature and Love in the Late Middle Ages* (Berkeley and Los Angeles, 1963), p. 179: he points out that Lydgate '. . . offers one of the most telling cases of monastic mentality and courtly attitudes in the same person: he was a monk and a courtly poet consistently, but distinctly'.

37 On the persistence of classical pictorialism in medieval literature, see J. H. Hagstrum, *The Sister Arts* (Chicago and London, 1958), pp. 37–56; on pictorialism in Chaucer see Hagstrum, *Sister Arts*, pp. 42–4, and M. Praz, *Mnemosine* (Milan, 1971), pp.

with 'many a faire image' (45) of lovers (47) 'Isette in ordre, aftir þei were trwe' (where *trwe* may also be taken to mean lifelike, exactly like), and this is a precise reference to the *Parliament*[38] and hence to the great master, Chaucer. All that remains for Lydgate to do is to *blot* and *spotte* – not to *peinte*. This new declaration of humility with regard to his art in fact gives us to understand his self-awareness as an authority on poetry.

The subject-matter of his poem is so difficult to express that it is clearly not enough to paint it with firm, regular, well-defined brush-strokes as the famous lovers in the temple of poetic tradition have been painted. This subject-matter must be rendered in a different way, by blotting, soiling and scoring. The Furies must drop their tears of unhappiness in the poet's ink that is about to stain the paper, in the sense of leaving traces on the paper of the unfortunate affair, after it has had its effect upon the eyelid. The subtle play on *pauper* thus takes us back again to the mirror metaphor since, in addition to paper and poetry, *pauper* (by way of a borrowed meaning from the French term) may also be read as 'eyelid'. And eyelid is a synecdoche for eye. The eye is no longer merely the organ reflecting the painted images, but is itself scored by the subject because this is a painful and a sinful one.[39]

This significant breach in the structure of the work is however immediately closed in the course of the narration where the lady tells the lover that the solution to their problem lies in waiting. In waiting for what? For her husband's death or total conformity to a stereotype of behaviour sanctioned by the code of chivalry? Just as the narrator/Venus defers the solution of the two lovers' plight to some future time, so the dreamer/narrator promises to write a 'litil tretise and a processe' (1380) in honour of women, and in so doing he repudiates the present poem as unfit to render the 'significaunce' of the dream itself.

The repetition of 'auisioun' and 'visioun' does not allude to something little more than a dream,[40] but to a dream that it is hard to explain but that the poet would like to see come true. In her first invocation to Venus the lady had stressed the division within herself between body

78–86, where, commenting on Chaucer's view of the world in the *Knight's Tale* as opposed to Dante's, Praz states: 'Dante presentava lo specchio a un mondo d'Eternità, Chaucer a uno di Mutabilità', p. 86.

38 *Parliament of Fowls*, ll. 284–94.

39 On the 'piercing eye motif' as the dominant metaphor of the *Temple of Glas* see A. Miskimin, 'Patterns in *The Kingis Quair* and the *Temple of Glas*', *Papers on Language & Literature* 13 (1977) 339–61, pp. 354–5. On the eye-as-mirror imagery cf. W. Deonna, *Le Symbolisme de l'Oeil* (Paris, 1965), especially pp. 290–300.

40 Norton-Smith, *J. Lydgate*, p. 191.

and mind and had given proof of the freedom of memory despite material hindrances.

The thesis that has been developed to this point is that a series of problems remains to be solved at the end of the dream/poem. This lack of solution, however, is what makes the work such an interesting one. Lydgate took on an extremely difficult job. He had in mind a whole tradition of courtly poetry as epitomized by the *Roman de la Rose* and accompanied by the linked commonplaces of service, feudal homage and adultery; but as a clerical intellectual (clerical against his will) he is inclined to moralize in all the literary genres he attempts.

The questions underlying the poem are rendered still more complicated by the division in the poet himself reflected by the lady: quite apart from the question of whether the poet and the dreamer are to be identified with each other or not,[41] there is a precise referent that is constantly present. This referent is desire, which, once revealed, is immediately denied. It is a double desire that the poet projects on to the two *personae* of the dream/poem. The desire of a real lover for a real woman is transferred to the *persona* of the lady and, as we have seen, she embodies the imbalance between full spiritual and physical enjoyment of love and the necessary compromise involved in an ideal adultery (which may allude to the conflict between marriage/artificial law and true love/natural law).[42]

The poet makes constant reference to the *auctores*, either naming them directly ('as Chaucer telliþ us' – 110) or referring to the 'image' (45), the painted representations of those famous lovers taken from famous classical authors. There is in all this a hint of a further desire on the part of the poet which is equally significant. The invocation to the Furies reveals his desire to present himself as an *auctor*. The painful subject the poet must treat is different, because it has been experienced by the poet himself, who has suffered all the anguish of a latent personal sin. It cannot therefore be presented in the same way as the classical pictures, because unlike them, it cannot be defined with firm outlines. It is spotted, and as such indefinable, incommunicable, shrouded in silence like the Furies.[43]

The analogy between the help the lady asks of Venus and the assistance the poet asks of the Furies receives support from the parallel be-

41 Norton-Smith, *J. Lydgate*, p. 179.
42 *Ibidem*.
43 On the representation of the Furies as silent in the 'Exclamacioun', see Norton-Smith, *J. Lydgate*, p. 129.

tween the interrelated stories of the poet and the lady, neither of which is concluded. The lady must wait, and the refinement of Lydgate's literary technique must await a future work. This work would perhaps be written in that aureate style he invented,[44] on a subject more suitable for moralizing. It would perhaps conform to the canons of the homily, the compilation or the epic, all 'safe' literary genres more to the taste of growing middle-class patronage.[45]

The structure of the framework could be seen as one of monotonous parallelism, but it contains the unexpected tensions of the *matere*. This situation is summed up emblematically in the title of the poem: the temple of glass. The poem is a sound and solid temple because it has its basis in Chaucer's poem, the great model that everyone looks to. It is a temple made of glass, however, which means that it is a reflecting and illuminating mirror.

> I purpose here to maken and to write
> A litil tretise and a processe make
> In pr[a]is of women, oonli for her sake,
> Hem to comende, as it is skil and riȝt,
> For here goodnes, with al my ful[le] myȝt. (1379–83)

The lady is the mirror of perfection and division, and the poem is the mirror of a past tradition. It is also, however, a mirror of personal tensions that the canons of the *stilus gravis* would have made it difficult to express. The poem, then, represents a 'new' image, even though the poet repudiates it with a rhetorical device.

44 On Lydgate's 'aureate' language, see J. C. Mendenhall, *Aureate Terms. A Study in the Literary Diction of the Fifteenth Century* (Lancaster, Pa., 1919); Schirmer, *J. Lydgate*, pp. 73–4 and L. Ebin, 'Lydgate's Views on Poetry', *Annuale Mediaevale* 18 (1977) 76–105; on the complex syntax of the *Temple of Glas*, see A. Courmont, *Studies on Lydgate's Syntax in the Temple of Glas* (Paris, 1912).

45 The first major work to follow the *Temple of Glas* is in fact *Resoun and Sensuallyte* based on a French model with a strong moral-philosophical interpretation. On patronage in the late Middle Ages, see R. F. Green, *Poets and Princepleasers: Literature and the English Court in the Late Middle Ages* (Toronto, 1980).

CHAPTER THREE

Specular Narrative: Hoccleve's *Regement of Princes*

Critical evaluation of Thomas Hoccleve as a mere imitator of Chaucer has had too long a currency,[1] and Hoccleve himself is partly to blame for this. His references to Chaucer are numerous. In the *Regement of Princes* he apostrophizes his 'maister' as 'flour of eloquence, / Mirour of fructuous entendement, / O, vniuersel fadir in science' (1962–4), and, using the *diminutio* technique, contrasts Chaucer's excellence with his own inability to express himself correctly: 'My yonge konyng may no hyer reche, / Mi wit is also slipir as an eel' (1984–5).

In recent years, however, critics like S. Medcalf and J. Burrow have stressed the autobiographical substratum – which thrusts itself to the surface in the Prologue and in the so-called *Series*[2] – that makes

1 Beginning with E. P. Hammond, *English Verse between Chaucer and Surrey* (Durham, North Carolina, 1927), pp. 53–6, who observes, however, that 'his constant tendency to the autobiographical is the most interesting of his qualities', p. 54, and up to J. Mitchell, *Thomas Hoccleve: A Study in Early Fifteenth-Century English Poetic* (Urbana, Illinois, 1968). On Chaucer's influence, see D. Pearsall, 'The English Chaucerians', in D. S. Brewer, ed., *Chaucer and Chaucerians* (London, 1966), pp. 222–5, and on his metrical debt to Chaucer, cf. I. Robinson, *Chaucer's Prosody* (Cambridge, 1971), pp. 190–9. Robinson points out that it is not technique but temperament that distances Hoccleve from Chaucer, p. 197. For a brief but fact-filled history of Hoccleve criticism, see the introduction in B. O'Donoghue, ed., *Thomas Hoccleve. Selected Poems* (Manchester, 1982), pp. 7–17.

The edition used throughout is F. J. Furnivall, ed., *Hoccleve's Works: III. The Regement of Princes and Fourteen of Hoccleve's Minor Poems*, EETS ES 72 (London, 1897); for the other minor poems the edition used is F. J. Furnivall and I. Gollancz, eds., *Hoccleve's Works: The Minor Poems*, EETS ES 61 and 73, 1892 and 1925, revised and reprinted as one volume by J. Mitchell and A. I. Doyle (London, 1970).

2 Medcalf in S. Medcalf, ed., *The Later Middle Ages* (London, 1981), pp. 124–40, quotes the impressions of a psychoanalyst as backing for his assertion of the autobiographical interest of Hoccleve's works, which may be considered as an account of the various phases of his depressive illness. J. Burrow examines Hoccleve criticism and analyses various meanings of the term 'autobiography' as applied to medieval and

Hoccleve's narrative uniquely his notwithstanding his observance of medieval conventions. His use of different literary genres, such as the petition that parodies the penitential lyric[3] in *La Male Regle* and the *consolatio*[4] in the Prologue and in the *Series* cannot prevent his readers from receiving an impression of 'modernity' from Hoccleve's poetry, especially when he offers them a minutely-detailed description of his deeply depressive state.[5]

Hoccleve's *Regement of Princes* is divided into two parts: the Prologue and the *Regement* proper. The Prologue has a quasi-typical dream setting. The poet cannot sleep: he is too worried about the world's problems and his own misfortunes. The next morning he goes out and meets an old beggar. They start a conversation, with Hoccleve showing moments of self-revelation and the Beggar trying to comfort the poet with long didactic sermons and by talking about his past life. At line 750 Hoccleve tells the Beggar about his melancholy. Being poor he fears for his old age. He then gives a detailed account of his work in the Privy Seal and of his annuity and complains about the troubles to which scribes are subject. After other allusions to his life, he laments the death of Chaucer, the flower of eloquence. Then the Beggar goes away and the poet announces that he will write a poem for Prince Henry.

At the beginning of the *Regement* proper, Hoccleve indicates his sources and refers again to Chaucer, whom he praises greatly. The *Rege-*

late medieval literature. He concludes that a careful examination of all Hoccleve's works 'implies, not only that Hoccleve really does talk about himself in his poetry, but also that his departures from the imaginary norm of simple autobiographical truth are themselves best understood by reflecting upon his particular circumstances' (J. A. Burrow, 'Autobiographical Poetry in the Middle Ages: The Case of Thomas Hoccleve', *Proceedings of the British Academy* 68 (1982) 389–412, p. 412. On recent bibliography and the *Series* see the two articles of respectively J. Mitchell, 'Hoccleve Studies, 1965–1981', pp. 49–63, and J. A. Burrow, 'Hoccleve's *Series*: Experience and Books', pp. 259–73, in R. F. Yeager, ed., *Fifteenth Century Studies: Recent Essays* (Hamden, Conn., 1984).

3 The analogy between themes present in the tradition of the penitential lyric and Hoccleve's poetry is shown in E. M. Thornley, 'The Middle English Penitential Lyric and Hoccleve's Autobiographical Poetry', *Neuphilologische Mitteilungen* 68 (1967) 295–321.

4 On the influence of Boethius, see, among others, P. B. R. Doob, *Nebuchadnezzar's Children: Conventions of Madness in Middle English Literature* (New Haven, Conn., 1974), pp. 216–19, where Hoccleve's obsessive preoccupation with physical and mental illness as a consequence of sin is particularly stressed (pp. 208–31).

5 Lewis, while he devotes very few lines to Hoccleve, yet associates him with Aeschylus for his skill in describing the anxiety of a man who is the prey to his own preoccupations, personified in Thought – C. S. Lewis, *The Allegory of Love* (Oxford, 1936), pp. 238–9.

ment was divided by the editor into fifteen sections named after the virtues that Hoccleve considers necessary for a king. The sections vary in length and in the number of the examples introduced to describe the various subjects. Personal allusions are also present, as in section 11 where he presses the prince for his annuity. The concluding section is on peace. To restore peace Hoccleve suggests the marriage of Prince Hal and the Princess of France.

The *Regement of Princes* is the work in which Hoccleve's personal history is allowed to merge most transparently with a theme of public importance, in this case the timeless history of princes. He achieves this blending by means of the mirror metaphor:[6] it is the way in which he juxtaposes two *specula* that constitutes the particular interest of the *Regement*. The Prologue is the mirror of Hoccleve's life for Prince Henry, and the *Regement* is the mirror of the good ruler,[7] i.e. Henry, for Hoccleve as subject and poet. By his own admission Hoccleve used three *auctoritates* ('Aristotle', Jacobus and Aegidius)[8] for his *speculum principis*, but he prefaces his treatise with the story of his life at the time of composing the *Regement*.

Hoccleve's attempt to put micro-history – his own life history – and macro-history – *exempla* for the prince – on the same plane becomes apparent when the structure and language of the two parts that make up the work are carefully examined. As Medcalf points out,[9] Hoccleve is firmly attached to the principles of order and planning set out by Geoffrey of Vinsauf in the *Poetria Nova* and celebrated by the narrator in Chaucer's *Troilus* (I, 1065–9). In the *Dialog* he asserts:

6 On metaphor frequency in general, cf. Mitchell, *T. Hoccleve*, p. 60.

7 On the mirror for the prince as a popular genre in fifteenth-century English literature, see D. Bornstein, 'Reflections of Political Theory and Political Fact in Fifteenth-Century Mirrors for the Prince', in J. B. Bessinger, Jr. and R. R. Raymo, eds., *Medieval Studies. In Honor of Lillian Herlands Hornstein* (New York, 1976), pp. 77–85. See also A. M. Kinghorn, *The Chorus of History. Literary-historical relations in Renaissance Britain* (London, 1971), ch. 11.

8 The texts used by Hoccleve are in fact the *Secreta Secretorum*, considered as a collection of Aristotle's admonitions to the young Alexander, Aegidius Romanus' *de Regimine Principum* and Jacobus de Cessolis' *Liber de Ludo Scaccorum*. On these sources of Hoccleve's see W. Matthews, 'Thomas Hoccleve', in A. E. Hartung, *A Manual of the Writings in Middle English 1050–1500*, iii (1972), pp. 903–8; A. H. Gilbert, 'Notes on the Influence of the *Secretum Secretorum*', *Speculum* 3 (1928) 84–98, especially pp. 93–8, and the introduction to the facsimile edition in N. F. Blake, ed., *Jacobus de Cessolis, The Game of Chess. Translated and printed by W. Caxton, c.1483* (London, 1976).

9 Medcalf, *The Later Middle Ages*, p. 131.

Thow woost wel / who shal an hous edifie,
Gooth nat ther-to withoute auisament,
If he be wys, for with his mental ye
ffirst is it seen / pourposid / cast & ment,
How it shal wroght been / elles al is shent.
Certes, for the deffaute of good forsighte,
Mis-tyden thynges / þat wel tyde mighte. (638–44)

It is to satisfy these principles of order and architectonic construction that Hoccleve juxtaposes the two parts in a play of reflected images, of analogies and dissimilarities. The length of the Prologue is in itself an indication of the importance Hoccleve wishes to give the dialogue between the first-person narrator and the Beggar, the wise old man who has learned life's lessons.

The opening of the poem is constructed according to the canons of the dream vision tradition.[10] The poet is worried, 'Mvsyng vpon the restles bisynesse / Which that this troubly world hath ay on honde' (1–2), and cannot sleep, because 'Thought' (7) keeps him awake. He adds that he has many a time suffered the same anguish and felt the need to flee the world to remain alone with himself, 'To sorwe soule, me thoght it dide me good' (91).

Constance Hieatt[11] holds that the structure of the dream-vision admits of a subdivision into four parts: Prologue, Break in Consciousness, Guidance and Epilogue. If this subdivision is applied to the *Regement*, Hoccleve's second part can be seen as a substantial modification. After the 'stormy nyght' (113) the poet wakes and, while walking through the fields, meets the Beggar – who is a character from real life. That he does not belong to the dream is made clear from his first words, 'Awake! & gan me schake wonder faste' (132), and ' "I," quod þis olde greye, / "Am heer" ' (134–5), almost as if to point out the necessity of distinguishing between the imaginary world created by the poet's oppressed mind and the everyday real world. Moreover, as we will see, Hoccleve is so taken up with his financial problems that he makes everything turn towards his own personal advantage, and here outer motives and inner reasons merge and mingle.

In his deeply depressive state Hoccleve shows from the very begin-

10 See P. Boitani, *English Medieval Narrative in the 13th & 14th Centuries* (Cambridge, 1982), ch. 4.

11 C. B. Hieatt, '*Un Autre Fourme*: Guillaume de Machaut and the Dream Vision Form', *Chaucer Review* 14 (1979) 97–115, especially pp. 105–8.

ning that he is certain of at least one thing: that his poetry is a possible stepping-stone to personal and social success. Unlike Skelton in the *Garlande of Laurell*, Hoccleve does not exalt his poetic craft, but, from the moment he meets the Beggar, he speculates on the value of writing and the possibility of exploiting it for his own ends. According to the Beggar, men of letters have 'gretter descrecioun' (155) and put their faith in 'resoun' (157), thus distancing themselves much more rapidly from 'folye' (158) than ignorant men who have no 'maner of lettrure' (160). Hoccleve gives weight to his role as a writer by quoting Chaucer as his master on many occasions: he declares that Chaucer is too exalted a model for others to imitate, but he nonetheless makes a direct association between his writings and Chaucer. Hoccleve goes even further: he passes over Lydgate and inserts himself after Chaucer and Gower as the third element in the literary triad, even though he does so to the accompaniment of yet another declaration of his inferiority. The Prologue ends on his expressed intention to write the Poem for Prince Henry.

Two characteristics, which are common to the two parts, emerge from a careful analysis of the structure of the Prologue both by itself and in connection with the actual *Regement*. These characteristics are, firstly, the close similarity between the *ordo* of the treatment of the subjects and, secondly, the affinity between Hoccleve's position and that of the future king. As regards the first element held in common, the Prologue is subdivided into: (1) Indication of the causes of the deeply depressive state; (2) Meeting with the guide, (2a) *Exempla* from the Bible and from contemporary society for didactic purposes (to fit Hoccleve's circumstances), (2b) Beggar's confession and repentance; (3) Hoccleve's life history with *exempla* from the Bible and from contemporary society, with no repentance but with a petition to Prince Henry. The *Regement* instead is subdivided into: (1) Proem with acknowledgment of the three authorities, 'Aristotle', Jacobus and Aegidius, whose words the author intends to transcribe into the vernacular for the future king's benefit; (2) Fifteen Sections given over to the virtues to practise and the vices to shun; (3) An Envoy with the customary reference to the inadequacy of the 'litell booke'.

The structural links between the *Regement* and the Prologue can be recognized in the content of the single sections. Section 11, entitled *De Virtute Largitatis & De Vicio Prodigalitatis*, is a case in point. The first part refers to 'Aristotil, of largesse' (4124), thus establishing the *auctoritas*. The second part consists of the *exemplum* of John of Canace, a very popular story in the Middle Ages, intended as a warning to Henry about when and how to distribute benefices. The novelty of the work, however, lies in the fact that it also connects the a-temporal nature of exemplification to Hoccleve's temporal condition. He admits he has been too prodigal with his money, yet, on this occasion just as in the Prologue, he fails to repent and immediately goes on to his petition to the prince. He admits 'I me repent of my mysrewly lyfe' (4376), but adds 'My yeerly guerdoun, myn annuite, / That was me graunted for my long labour, / Is al behynde, I may naght payed be' (4383–5). The originality of Hoccleve's *speculum* lies, then, in his going on from his own impoverished condition to the likelihood of the king's own destruction if he allows himself to be pressed into distributing benefices by the bad advice of his flatterers. Hoccleve is aware of the irony of his position as a petitioner[12] presenting a book to obtain money. He asserts, however, that his sole purpose in writing is to add to the 'renoun' of the prince, seeing that his words are dictated by good faith.[13] Hoccleve hits out at flatterers in an attempt to persuade the king to loosen his purse-strings for the poor scribe's benefit.

The short section 13, *De regis prudencia*, where Hoccleve deals with the customary commonplace of the moral virtues to be cultivated, is another example of structural likeness. Hoccleve addresses the prince directly, urging him 'Be prudent, as þat þe scripture vs lereth' (4752) and thus quoting his *auctoritas*. Of moral virtues the sovereign must possess above all prudence, by the light of which he will be enabled to observe 'in euery herne / Of þynges past, and ben, & þat schul be' (4765–6).[14] The poet continues talking about the necessity for prudence and then falls at once into the usual pattern of associating the king's conduct with his own condition, although this time the allusion is indirect. In reality, Hoccleve implores the future king to keep the agreements he has put his seal to, taking the pensions granted to subjects as an example: 'Now, if þat ye graunten by your patente / To your seruauntes a yeerly guerdoun, / Crist scheelde þat your wil or your entente / Be sette to maken a

12 On the circulation and the importance of petitions in Hoccleve's time see A. L. Brown, *The Privy Seal in the Early Fifteenth Century* (D.Phil. thesis, Oxford, 1954), ch. II. See also R. F. Green, *Poets and Princepleasers: Literature and the English Court in the Late Middle Ages* (Toronto, 1980), pp. 42–3 and J. A. Burrow, 'The Poet as Petitioner', *Studies in the Age of Chaucer* 3 (1981) 61–75.

13 *Regement*: ll. 4399–403.

14 On the portrayal of Prudence as triple-faced as well as double-faced in the iconography of the fourteenth and fifteenth centuries, see H. Schwarz, 'The Mirror in Art', *The Art Quarterly* 15 (1952) 97–118, especially pp. 104–5.

restriccioun / Of paiement' (4789–93). In this case too the obsessive reference to the failure to pay his stipend appears.

In the last section, entitled *Of Peace*, which is the most 'public' part of the *Regement* in that Hoccleve here declares himself in favour of the fusion of the royal houses of England and France through Henry and Catherine's marriage,[15] the motif of the two evils the sovereign must avoid, Avarice and Flattery, is introduced. These evils lead back inevitably to Hoccleve's situation. On one hand Avarice (embodied in the Roman *populus*) puts 'profyte singuler' (5249) before 'profyt commun' (5250) – the implication here is that the sovereign thinks neither of the people's welfare nor of Hoccleve's tranquillity; on the other, Flattery rules over the country to the exent that the livings and the various ecclesiastical benefices go to the flatterers rather than to the Oxford and Cambridge 'worthi clerk famouse' (5272), i.e., the intellectuals do not receive privileges worthy of their reputation, and Hoccleve too is damaged by this situation. Hoccleve's intention to relate the various issues to himself is therefore evident. Hoccleve introduces commonplaces familiar to the public into the *Regement* and these allow him to locate his poem within a well-defined tradition that can be traced through Boethius, the *psychomachia* and the *specula principum*. He modifies this tradition, however, in terms of his own self, by setting his own story and that of the prince side by side.

As we have already seen, the structure of the dream vision poem has been maintained almost intact,[16] even if the basic premise, the dream itself, is lacking. The subject on which it is centred is a commonplace handed down from Boethius – how to parry Fortune's blows – but this is paradoxically whittled down to a single opposition that was vital for Hoccleve: poverty/material well-being. Hoccleve endeavours to camouflage this obsession of his – the fruit, certainly, of an objective situation – by using the genres with the widest circulation for the purposes of his

15 On the question of peace through union of the two kingdoms of France and England, cf. R. P. Adams, 'Pre-Renaissance Courtly Propaganda for Peace in English Literature', *Papers of the Michigan Academy* 32 (1946) 431–46, especially pp. 440–3; Bornstein, 'Reflections of Political Theory', pp. 81–2. On dual monarchy in the reign of Henry VI, see J. W. McKenna, 'Henry VI of England and the Dual Monarchy: Aspects of Royal Political Propaganda, 1422–1432', *Journal of the Warburg and Courtauld Institutes* 28 (1965) 145–63, especially pp. 145–53.

16 On the popularity of dream poetry among middle-class readers, cf. W. F. Schirmer, *John Lydgate. A Study in the Culture of the XVth Century*, trans. A. E. Keep (Westport, Conn., 1961), pp. 36–7. In addition see P. Strohm's interesting article, 'Chaucer's Audience', *Literature and History* 5 (1977) 26–41, which, although it deals with the public reached by Chaucer, can also be partly applied to Hoccleve.

petition. In this operation Hoccleve shows himself to be very skilful. Just as a figure of consolation appeared to Boethius, so the Old Beggar appears to Hoccleve. This Beggar, while he allows him to put all the available commonplaces on show, neither consoles him nor induces him to repent. Like the Beggar, Hoccleve has sinned, but the central problem, the cause of all the ills that beset him, is not sin alone but above all lack of money:

> It goht ful streite and scharp or I it haue;
> If I seur were of it be satisfied
> ffro yeer to yeer, than, so god me saue,
> My deepe rootid grief were remedied
> Souffissantly; but how I schal be gyed
> Heer-after, whan þat I no lenger serue,
> This heuyeth me, so þat I wel ny sterue. (827–33)

In the two parts of the *Regement*, the motif of the need for material well-being recurs again and again, and in this way traditionally allegorical themes and motifs are subjected to a *de facto* secularization. The poem reveals the considerable influence of morality-play subject matter. One might even say that Hoccleve anticipates what Skelton was to do in *Magnyfycence*, where he combines precepts for the prince with an attack on his sworn enemy, Wolsey. Here Hoccleve keeps a thematic and structural distinction between the two parts, the Prologue and the *speculum*, even though this distinction is more apparent than real. Unlike Skelton, he does not hurl invective. However, what I have said in the foregoing pages gives an idea of how the poet endeavours to exploit for his own individual purposes the Boethian theory of opposites,[17] and together with this the tradition of allegorical personifications of evil which were already in the process of dramatic transformation towards more realistic presentation in the morality play.[18]

According to Diane Bornstein,[19] the main interest of the *Regement* lies in the fact that Hoccleve deals with the problems that the men of his times felt most keenly, such as absenteeism, adultery, injustice and corruption, but this is no more than standard practice, seeing that he is writing an *exemplum* for the prince's benefit. Instead, the real focus of

17 *De Consolatione Philosophiae* IV, pr. 2.

18 Cf. A. Torti, 'La funzione dei "Vizi" nella struttura del *Morality Play* del Primo Periodo Tudor', *Annali della Facoltà di Lettere e Filosofia dell' Università di Perugia* 14 (1976–1977) 177–217.

19 Bornstein, 'Reflections of Political Theory', p. 81.

interest is in the emphasis given to the role of the poet and his ability to manipulate literary tradition in favour of his petition. Boethius is certainly the authority the Prologue refers to and *De Consolatione Philosophiae* the work taken by Hoccleve as his model, to judge from the opening to the poem:

> And how in bookes thus I wryten fynde,
> 'The werste kynde of wrecchednesse is,
> A man to have been weelfull or this.' (54–6)

Immediately prior to these lines, however, Hoccleve establishes the opposition that will be the referent for the two parts:

> I seey weel povert was exclusion
> Of all weelfare regnyng in mankynde. (52–3)

This opposition, which is formally of a moral nature but was in fact realistically present in Hoccleve's life, is connected with the structure of the morality play. Here the opposition is fall/salvation, the fall caused by the vices (especially certain vices) and salvation due to the grace of God, by means of the help the virtues confer on man.[20]

At this point it is interesting to see what vices Hoccleve intends taking as his target, and what virtues are to be practised. Just as the slow process of secularization of the drama was reducing the figures of evil and centring their role in a particular vice,[21] so in Hoccleve's poem the two evils considered to be worst with reference to the prince and to his people are Flattery and Avarice. On the other hand the virtues that the common people (in the Prologue) and the prince (in the *Regement*) must cultivate are Chastity, Humility, Prudence, etc., all of which tend towards the well-being of the sovereign but also of his subjects.

Both formally and thematically the poem has a circular structure, as the play of symmetries and variations shows. In the Prologue Hoccleve is consumed by anxiety and cannot rest; he then meets the Beggar, whose tale relates to the poet's past life and indicates the vices to shun and the

20 On the structure of the morality play, see the excellent, still valid introduction to the edition of *Magnyfycence* in R. L. Ramsay, ed., *Magnyfycence, by J. Skelton*, EETS ES 98 (London, 1908); see also E. N. S. Thompson, 'The English Moral Play', *Transactions of the Connecticut Academy of Arts and Sciences* 14 (1910) 291–414.

21 In *The Castle of Perseverance*, the oldest morality play in English that has come down to us with an unmutilated text and the whole range of vices and virtues, one among the Seven Deadly Sins, Covetousness, dominates all the others on stage.

virtues to practise; and finally there is the announcement that he will write a poem for Henry. In the *Regement* Hoccleve proposes to put together the stories he has found in his three authorities, and hopes that

> Yf þat you liste of stories to take hede,
> Somwhat it may profite, by your leve:
> At hardest, when þat ye ben in Chambre at eve,
> They ben goode to drive forth the nyght;
> They shull not harme, yf þey be herd a-right. (2138–42)

He makes didactic use of the stories that refer to real or imaginary happenings involving sovereigns of past ages, and finally there is the Envoy to the book that has been completed, and which begins with the sleepless night. The circular structure of both the Prologue and the *Regement* can be described in synthesis as follows:

Prologue — Hoccleve's sleeplessness and the uselessness of his tale. Beggar's *exempla* (need for virtue). Usefulness of the poet's writing (Chaucer's help).

Regement — Prince's sleeplessness and the usefulness of Hoccleve's tale. *Exempla* for the prince (need for wealth, for himself and his subjects; need for virtue). Chaucer's sanctification. Appeal both for internal pacification and external pacification with France. The book ends with a section dedicated to peace.

The complexity and symmetry of the structure show how deeply aware Hoccleve is, even when he denies it, of his role as poet. As such he is able to imitate the great authors of the past – and he adds quite openly that he may be able to make practical use of his writing. Hoccleve then uses the most traditional of genres and themes, but what he is really stressing is that certain values from the past, valid though they may still be, are less impelling than they once were. In the final analysis the *psychomachia* is reduced to the struggle between poverty and riches, these riches being individual and social welfare. Like the *Regement, Piers Plowman* suggested equality and social justice as the starting point for spiritual salvation, but Hoccleve seems to attach a different importance to the two poles. There are many episodes in the *Regement* – like the story of John of Canace – that urge the sovereign not to place his trust in transient riches. However, John of Canace's story relates to Hoccleve's poverty if the prince does not pay him his annuity, even though the poet hints at his folly and repentance: 'I me repent of my mysrewly lyfe; / Wherfor, in þe wey of sauacioun / I hope I be' (4376–8); and it is the conclusion to this story that reveals how material well-being is considered as important as spiritual well-being, and that the intellectual, like the rest of the king's servants, has a right to a just reward. The identification and denunciation of the social ills of his time serve Hoccleve's purpose, which is to show the need to eliminate poverty, and so attain to a more acceptable standard of living. This does not mean that Hoccleve is a kind of Everyman, an emblem of humanity as a whole, but rather that he, like all men, has a right to survive. As a poet his right is to have patrons that protect him by holding his work in due esteem and saving him from ruining his eyesight as a scribe.[22] In order to explain the reasons for a lack of social justice he uses what were destined to become the worst sins a century later, in the full reawakening of humanism – Flattery and Avarice in close connection. That the account of the ills that threaten his subjects, and Hoccleve in particular, anticipates and is then incorporated into the description of the ills that the sovereign must avoid inflicting on his subjects and on Hoccleve himself, is a demonstration of the specular nature of the two parts of the poem.

Both in the Prologue and in the *Regement* Flattery and Avarice join forces to lead man to wretchedness. In those who embody these sins this wretchedness will be of a moral kind; in those who are subjected to the effects of these sins, it will be material. In the Prologue the Flatterer is described by the Beggar as a man dressed in costly, sumptuous clothes; only by eliminating the squandering of money induced by Pride will there be more for the people: 'Than myghte siluer walke more thikke / Among þe peple þan þat it doþ now' (526–7). Hoccleve is alluding to the fact that the Lords are lavish with money for their own interests, but not equally so for the benefit of their subjects. Towards the end of the Prologue, after Hoccleve's insistence on the need for a regular stipend, the Beggar reintroduces the theme of the flattery the Lords, unaware of their unpopularity, are subject to. In the Prologue, therefore, the Lords' flattery towards the king and the king's avarice towards the people combine to bring about the ruin, that is, the material poverty of the

22 On the complex relationship between poets and court in the late Middle Ages, see Green, *Poets and Princepleasers*. In his capacity as clerk of the Privy Seal, Hoccleve was not in a very high social position, as R. F. Green shows in his essay 'The *Familia Regis* and the *Familia Cupidinis*', in V. J. Scattergood and J. W. Sherborne, eds., *English Court Culture in the Later Middle Ages* (London, 1983), 87–108, p. 106. On Hoccleve's work as scribe, cf. H. C. Schulz, 'Thomas Hoccleve, Scribe', *Speculum* 12 (1937) 71–81 and A. Compton Reeves, 'Thomas Hoccleve, Bureaucrat', *Medievalia et Humanistica* 5 (1974) 201–14.

people and of the poet in particular. While the Prologue is characterized by the emphasis on the poet's personal situation, the *Regement* stresses above all the vices to be shunned, and this is the case even in the sections dedicated to a single virtue. It is here that Flattery and Avarice assume a principal role. As early as the fourth section, *On Observing of the Laws*, there is the description of the Flatterers who have already made a place for themselves at court and prevent the Lords from acting justly:

> But certes, fauel hath caght so sad foote
> In lordes courtes, he may naght þens slyde;
> Who com or go, algate abyde he moote;
> His craft is to susteyne ay þe wrong syde;
> And fro vertu his lorde to devide. (2941–5)

There is also here an insistence on the division, in this case inner division, which adulation effects; this will lead to social division and hence to civil war. Further on, in *De Pietate* (section 5), Hoccleve hurls wrathful invective at the Flatterers:

> ffor þu hast neuer þi lordys estate
> To herte chere, but al þi bysynesse
> Is for þi lucre, and þi cofres warmnesse. (3057–9)

In language taken from the world of commerce he compares them to blind merchants:

> O ffauel! a blynde marchant art þou oone,
> That, for wordly goode, & grace and fauoure . (3074–5)

From the ninth to the fifteenth section Hoccleve exploits the examples taken from the *auctores* to show the connection between Flattery and Avarice. Given that for Avarice there is no remedy (section 12) and that it is 'Roote of al harmes, fo to conscience' (4734), it is against this evil that the king must take precautions. He must practise the opposite virtue, that is, generosity, liberality, if he has his people's good at heart:

> . . . a kyng moot algates flee
> A chynches herte, for his honeste
> And for þe profyte, as I seide aboue,
> Of his peple, if he þynke wynne here loue. (4659–62)

Section 11, dedicated to liberality (and also to its abuse, prodigality) lays stress on the king's not giving heed to the Flatterers: he must follow the advice of his true counsellors and know how to make a correct choice of men to give to and the amounts to give them. Seeing that Hoccleve is asking the king for the payment of his annuity, his way of relating the general question of the liberality of the king to his personal problem as an individual and as a poet is evident. The fact is that he intends to be paid not only for his 'long labour' (4384), but also for the book he is writing (and for other works he has already written). The book in hand will serve to increase the king's 'renoun' (4400) and is dictated by good faith. In section 13, headed *De regis prudencia*, he returns to the subject of the payment of pensions, which a king must keep up if he wishes to retain his people's confidence. He deals with this subject indirectly, but he uses the same terms 'yeerly guerdoun' (4790). The close connection between Flattery and Avarice is repeated in section 14, and here Hoccleve advises the prince to avoid both these most dangerous evils:

> In auxenge eeke of reed, ware of fauel;
> Also ware of þe auariciouse;
> ffor none of þo two can conseile wel;
> Hir reed & conseil is envenymouse;
> Þei bothe ben of golde so desirous,
> Þei rekke naght what bryge her lorde be Inne,
> So þat þei mowen golde & siluyr wynne. (4915–21)

The conclusion to be drawn from the foregoing is that the attack on Flattery and Avarice is no mere expression of a traditional attitude to two allegorical personifications whose negative role had already been brought out in the morality plays; it is above all an attack that Hoccleve makes on the inordinately powerful members of the *camera regis*:[23] these give the sovereign bad counsel, and he makes no objection. Hoccleve does not stop at a simple description of the ills of his time but suggests an alternative: in time of peace as in time of war the king must be counselled by elderly men and not young ones, who often prove to be foolhardy. At this point he introduces the 'sanctification' of Chaucer,[24] who

23 On the role of the king's chamber in the late Middle Ages, see Green, *Poets and Princepleasers*, especially ch. 2.

24 On the importance of the iconographic representation of Chaucer in the *Regement* and on Chaucer's role as a sort of prototype counsellor of princes, see J. H. McGregor's interesting article, 'The Iconography of Chaucer in Hoccleve's *De Regimine Principum* and in the *Troilus* frontispiece', *Chaucer Review* 11 (1976–77) 338–50.

is invoked as 'The firste fyndere of our faire langage' (4978), 'my fadir' (4982), 'My worthi maister Chaucer' (4983).[25] The terms used are connected with the terms in which Hoccleve's previous recommendation of elderly, expert counsellors was couched. The question raised here is what Chaucer's presence, iconographic though it may be, signifies in this part of the work.

In the first place, Chaucer is recalled as an author of sacred texts, in particular of prayers to the Virgin Mary. Then there is his portrayal in colours, as a permanent reminder for those who have perhaps forgotten him and in opposition to those who argue that images are false. Hoccleve stresses the positive value of holy images, because

> . . . whan a þing depeynt is,
> Or entailed, if men take of it heede,
> Thoght of þe lyknesse, it wil in hem brede. (5003–5)

In this way he creates an association between the picture of Chaucer and likenesses of the saints, thus making of Chaucer's image an object of adoration. Just as the Beggar recalled Hoccleve's friendship with the great Chaucer in the Prologue – to the accompaniment of professions of modesty on the poet's part – so the figure of Chaucer, father and master, stands out, iconographically, at the end of the *Regement*. Chaucer's 'sanctification' is placed directly after the admonition to the king to take heed of older counsellors and before the reference to the limitations of his book:

> More othir þing, wolde I fayne speke & touche
> Heere in þis booke; but such is my dulnesse –
> ffor þat al voyde and empty is my pouche, –
> Þat al my lust is queynt with heuynesse,
> And heuy spirit comaundith stilnesse. (5013–17)

In this way Hoccleve justifies his own writing, putting his work, inadequate though it may be, in relation to the master, who is also the symbol of the type of counsellor a king should give heed to.[26] Thus the reference to those who have perhaps forgotten the master may be read as a specu-

[25] On the difficult Chaucerian heritage received by his fifteenth-century followers, see the enlightening essay by A. C. Spearing, 'Chaucerian Authority and Inheritance', in P. Boitani and A. Torti, eds., *Literature in Fourteenth-Century England* (Tübingen and Cambridge, 1983), pp. 185–202, especially pp. 199–202.

[26] Cf. McGregor, 'The Iconography of Chaucer', pp. 342–5.

lar allusion, which relates to the reality under Hoccleve's eyes: he is an honest labourer who, unlike the farmer, uses a pen; he deserves to be paid for what he does, because his work as an intellectual is performed in good faith, for the prince's honour, with as guide and mentor the poet who was the first to join the tradition of the classical writers. 'Aristotle', Jacobus and Aegidius are his *auctoritates*, and he can benefit by their example because he has been a disciple in direct contact (as he asserts) or in indirect contact with the teachings of Chaucer.

This is not the end of the *Regement*, however, even though Hoccleve considers the following section (15, *Of Peace*) as a corollary and a hoped-for condition of moral and material tranquillity that would favour writing:

> And haue I spoke of pees, I schal be stille;
> God sende vs pees, if þat it be his wille. (5018–19)

In this concluding section Hoccleve indicates on the one hand the causes of civil and foreign wars, and on the other expresses his hope for peace as the fruit of man's spiritual life, from which material peace may ensue. Stanza 723 is highly autobiographical, contrasting as it does the state of tranquillity of men at peace with themselves with the terrible state of a man without peace of mind, a man identifiable with the poet himself:

> The thrid is eke tranquillite of þought,
> Þat gydeth man to pees; for as a wight
> May in a bedde of þornes reste noght,
> Riȝt so, who is with greuous þoughtes twight,
> May with himself nor othir folk a-riȝt
> Haue no pees; a man mot nedys smert
> When irous þoughtes occupye his hert. (5055–61)

Here 'tranquillite of þought' is in contrast with 'greuous þoughtes' and 'irous þoughtes', which refer back to the beginning of the Prologue, when the poet tossed and turned in bed, a prey to disquietude. The image of the bed returns as a synecdoche in the following stanza:

> And euene as vppon a pillow softe,
> Man may him reste wele, and take his ese,
> Riȝt so þat lorde þat sittith in heuen a-lofte,
> Herte peisible can so like and plese. (5062–5)

In the Prologue the poet's sleeplessness, which has his spiritual and material insecurity at its root, is described with sea metaphors expressing instability, such as 'And when I hadde rolled vp and doun / This worldes stormy wawes in my mynde' (50–1), 'Þe þoghtful wight is vessel of turment' (81), and 'Passe ouer whanne þis stormy nyght was gon' (113). Here instead the state of tranquillity that his inner peace has created suggests images of stability associated with the house: 'To crist ordeyneþ he a mancioun, / Which in his hertes habitacioun' (5023–4) and 'In place of pees, resteth our saviour' (5068).

Heart's ease and civil peace are however a hardly attainable Utopia while Flattery and Avarice still reign, and Hoccleve is obliged to admit:

> Þis is no doute, þat ambicioun
> And couetyse fyre al þis debate;
> Tho two be of wikked condicioun. (5223–5)

> By-hold how auarice crepith inne,
> And kyndlith werre, and quenchiþ vnite!
> O fauel! þou myghtest ben of hir kynne, (5251–3)

The two vices are the cause of inner division ('This fauel is of pees a destourbour; / Twix god and mannes soule he werre reisith;' – 5258–9) and war between Christian nations ('Alase! Also, þe greet dissencioun, / The pitous harme, þe hateful discorde, / Þat hath endured twix þis regioun / And othir landes cristen!' – 5314–17). It is the insatiable hungering after wealth that is the cause of war, and war's effects are devastating for society as a whole:

> What cornes wast, and doune trode & schent!
> How many a wif and maide haþ be by layn!
> Castels doun bette, and tymbred houses brent,
> And drawen downe, and al to-torne and rent! (5336–9)

Certain categories, like the 'worthi clerk famouse' (5272) and 'The knyght or sqwier, on þat other syde, / Or Ieman' (5279–80) are particularly hard hit by the injustices to which Avarice and Flattery give rise.

The poet has no need to refer to famous examples from the past to illustrate the ills of division and warfare. The disasters are there for everyone to see:

Now vnto my mateere of werre inwarde
Resort I; but to seke stories olde
Non nede is, syn þis day sharp werre & harde
Is at þe dore here, as men may be-holde. (5286–9)

In the Prologue Hoccleve establishes the space-time co-ordinates with particular accuracy, giving his location 'At Chestre ynne, right fast be the stronde' (5), insisting on the sequence of sleepless nights, and then specifying the events of *one particular night* and *the day* of his meeting with the Beggar. Similarly, at the end of the *Regement*, in the Epilogue, he makes use of the Hundred Years' War between France and England and of the state of civil strife by way of exemplification.

Like most dream poems, this work too has a circular structure,[27] in that the epilogue refers back to the prologue: if social peace is an impossibility, there is no hope of individual peace. Assuming unity to be a basic element of peace, then the marriage of the king with Catherine of France (which was indeed celebrated in 1420) would open the way to a fusion of the two nations, France and England, and might ensure lasting peace and the people's welfare as its consequence:

Purchaseth pees by wey of mariage,
And ye þerinne schul fynden auauntage. (5403–4)

With these lines Hoccleve's obsession comes to the surface again: he considers the attainment of material well-being as the solution to all his problems.

The structural circularity of the *Regement* is made clear by the repetition, at the end, of subject-matter expressed in the same terms as are to be found at the beginning of the Prologue. In the meditation that foreshadows the meeting with the Beggar the most frequently used terms are 'poverte', 'povert', 'thoght' ('Who so þat thoghty is, is wo-be-gon' – 80), as well as terms alluding to inner division – 'Þe place eschewit he where as ioye is, / ffor ioye & he not mowe accorde a-ryght; / As discordant as day is vn-to nyught'; 94–6. In the last section the three components of peace, 'Conformyng in god', 'in our self humblesse' and 'And with our neigheboures tranquillite' (5035–6) are described in

27 On the circular structure of *Pearl*, for example, see '*Pearl*: the circle as figural space', in C. Nelson, *The Incarnate Word. Literature as Verbal Space* (Urbana, Chicago and London, 1973), pp. 25–49.

terms of 'concorde' (5032) and 'vnite' (5054), which may be read on both the individual and social plane.

In this way Hoccleve very skilfully induces the reader to connect the question of civil peace with man's inner peace. But the individual man who is the direct and indirect subject of the speeches of the two *personae* in the Prologue, the poet and the Beggar, is Thomas Hoccleve, product of a sinful life that has reduced him to penury, but victim also of the unjust workings of the court, which often reward the unworthy and disregard the efforts and usefulness of the intellectual. If society is divided, this division and the resulting lack of security have their repercussions on the intellectual, who cannot write because

> A writer mot thre thynges to hym knytte,
> And in tho may be no disseuerance;
> Mynde, ee, and hand, non may fro othir flitte,
> But in hem mot be ioynt continuance. (995–8)

If a man's thoughts are taken up with economic worries, he cannot concentrate on his writing.

The mirror of Hoccleve's life (which is also reflected in the tale of the Beggar's life) is joined to the mirror of the prince's life (for which the histories of the powerful are the image). Both mirrors function positively and negatively, with vices to shun and virtues to practise. The term 'mirour' is used by Hoccleve twice only in this structural sense:[28] the first instance is at the end of the Prologue and the reference is to Chaucer, 'Mirour of fructuous entendement' (1963); the second is a reference to the governments of France and England at the end of the *Regement*, 'Yeue hem ensamplen! ye ben hir mirrours' (5328). The peoples of France and England must see themselves reflected in their rulers, as Hoccleve, because he is a poet, must see himself reflected in his master, Chaucer. The correlation Hoccleve → Chaucer and people → sovereign can also be read as Hoccleve ↔ people and Chaucer ↔ sovereign, for Hoccleve, as we have seen, seems to imply an allusion to the need to place intellectual and ruler on the same plane.

The mainspring of the poet's writing is his concern about ways and means to solve his pressing everyday financial problems. He goes beyond this aim, however, to the point of asserting that the welfare of the nation

28 If exception is made for verse 1441: 'Hem hoghte to be mirours of sadnesse', referring to Parsons who give themselves up to lustful living instead of cultivating humilty and moral virtue.

depends on a state of peace, and that the sovereign must preserve this peace with the support of able counsellors fulfilling their purpose of constant moral admonition.[29] As the 45 extant manuscripts of the *Regement* itself attest, the literary genre of the *speculum* was very popular in Hoccleve's time, and he exploits it to these ends.[30]

In conclusion, the interest of Hoccleve's work lies in the close connection between the first and second parts, the Prologue and the *Regement*, and in the 'new' use of literary genres and traditional commonplaces. On the one hand the poet uses the Prologue, the more personal part, to exalt his role as writer in its most laborious and painful aspects, and the *Regement* to show his skill in putting his literary ability to good account in a work designed to suit the widespread taste for tradition. On the other hand, as I have attempted to show, his use of the conventions is very different. There are all the most fashionable literary genres from the dream vision to the *speculum principis*, but these are copied in different ways and to a greater or lesser degree to tie in with Hoccleve's personal history. Thus there are descriptions of illness and social satire both in the Prologue and the *Regement* together with moral reflections on Hoccleve's own life and on the events of contemporary history, from the Lollard movement[31] to the greed and injustice of men at court. All these elements, however, bear the hallmark of the author's strong personality. Thus not even the sections of exemplification in the *Regement* can be considered a catalogue of more or less famous stories drawn out with the *amplificatio* technique that Lydgate was to master both in the *Troy Book* and in the *Fall of Princes*; on the contrary, there *are* these exemplary stories, but their purpose is continually to draw the future king's attention to the present – often Hoccleve's own present.

The aim of every *speculum* is certainly to advise the prince, or ruler in general, against falling into the errors of past rulers, errors which could lead ultimately to the ruin of the prince himself and of his people. The novelty of the *Regement* lies in the close connection between the prince's education and the poet's personal situation. The ills of early fifteenth-century English society are brought continually under the future king's eyes with their devastating effects: the concentration of benefices in the hands of the ecclesiastics, the greed of the gentry, the prevailing injustice that caused the old soldiers of the French wars to be

29 Cf. McGregor, 'The Iconography of Chaucer', p. 342.
30 See Green, *Poets and Princepleasers*, especially ch. 5.
31 On Hoccleve's attacks on the Lollards, also in the 'Address to Sir John Oldcastle', cf. Green, *Poets and Princepleasers*, pp. 183–6.

forgotten, just like the 'clerkes' of Oxford and Cambridge. Both Lydgate and Hoccleve are authors of long poems, but if one may complain of the lack of invention and structure in the former,[32] the situation is different with the latter. He can be credited with considerable skill in knitting the two parts of the work together with parallels and dissimilarities so as to allow a mirror reading.

Specularity normally permits the presence of reality in a literary text[33] only by means of allusion, but in the *Regement*, Hoccleve's tales, mirroring each other, finally return the reader to the reality of the poet's own life – or at least the fictional account of it. Thus the poet's wretched situation in the present is reflected retrospectively in the past life of the old man, and the parallel 'complaints' for the soldiers and intellectuals at the beginning and end of the work respectively relate to the double role that Hoccleve is trying to assume at court, that of professional writer[34] and therefore worker, and that of poet whose originality can achieve the fusion of his personal anxieties with the traditional presentation of *exempla* for the future sovereign. And Hoccleve's achievement is all the more to be commended in that he has succeeded, not without some stylistic weaknesses and certainly with obsessive references to his lack of means, in communicating the effort needed to write, and in addition to this, the essential role of the intellectual, in a court given over to corruption, by the side of a sovereign who must abandon his policy of warfare and ensure lasting peace. Peace will bring in its train social and individual tranquillity, which is the first essential for economic prosperity and for the inner harmony Hoccleve needs to be able to write.

32 D. Pearsall, *Gower and Lydgate* (London, 1969), p. 27.

33 On textual specularity, from Homer to modern literature, see Françoise Létoublon's article, 'Le miroir et la boucle', *Poétique* 53 (1983) 19–36, especially pp. 21–4.

34 On the possibility of Henry V's having commissioned Hoccleve to write the Address to Oldcastle as a form of propaganda against the Lollards, see Green, *Poets and Princepleasers*, pp. 185–6.

CHAPTER FOUR

Reality – Mirror – Allegory: John Skelton

John Skelton is a very difficult author to define and for this reason he has been labelled from one critical standpoint as completely medieval and from another as a forerunner of the new cultural climate of the Renaissance. His life spans the end of the fifteenth and the beginning of the sixteenth century; except however for his taking the side of the conservatives with regard to the teaching of Latin, he does not seem to have been affected by More's and Erasmus' concern with a new kind of education and a new role for the intellectual in society. His works are classified both as personal satire (because of his persistent anti-Wolsey obsession)[1] and as allegorical narrative (because of his return to the dream-vision tradition in some of his more significant long poems).[2]

An analysis of the structure and language of two of his fundamental works, *The Bowge of Courte* and *Speke Parott*,[3] can contribute to the understanding of this complex, many-sided author. The choice of these

1 On the possibility of interpreting Skelton's work in terms of the tradition of satire, see A. R. Heiserman, *Skelton and Satire* (Chicago, 1961) and P. D. Psilos, ' "Dulle" Drede and the Limits of Prudential Knowledge in Skelton's *Bowge of Courte*', *The Journal of Medieval and Renaissance Studies* 6 (1976) 297–317. On satire in general, cf. A. Brilli, ed., *La Satira. Storia, tecniche e ideologie della rappresentazione* (Bari, 1979).

2 S. J. Kozikowski, 'Allegorical Meanings in Skelton's *The Bowge of Courte*', *Philological Quarterly* 61 (1982) 305–15, analyses the influence that the dream allegory tradition had on Skelton. See also J. M. Berdan, *Early Tudor Poetry 1485–1547* (New York, 1931), pp. 95–8 and A. Swallow, 'John Skelton: The Structure of the Poem', *Philological Quarterly* 32 (1953) 29–42, p. 31. J. S. Larson, 'What is the *Bowge of Courte*?', *Journal of English and Germanic Philology* 61 (1962) 288–95, holds that the poem is a parody of medieval allegory. M. Pollet, *John Skelton: Poet of Tudor England* (London, 1971) and I. A. Gordon, *John Skelton. Poet Laureate* (Melbourne and London, 1943) see Skelton as a transitional poet between the Middle Ages and Humanism.

3 The edition of Skelton's poems I have used is *John Skelton: The Complete English Poems*, ed. J. Scattergood (Harmondsworth, 1983); *John Skelton. Poems*, ed. R. S. Kinsman (Oxford, 1969) has also been taken into consideration.

two works, at a first reading very different from each other, is motivated, as we will see, by thematic similarity.

As I have already mentioned, and as many critics have noted,[4] Skelton makes use of material taken from Chaucer and the Chaucerians. In his hands this material takes a different shape, but his poetry is not unambiguously forward-looking. It is certainly, however, the sign of a crisis in values and of the impossibility of presenting this crisis in traditional language, which explains the need to experiment with new forms of expression.

Drede's inability to see through and guard against the subtle guile of the Tudor court, the components of this trickery being personified in morality play characters, leads us to an awareness of the desolation of England brought about by the abuses of the age. It is Parott who denounces these abuses in accordance with the classical figure of prosopopoeia. Drede, with all his 'lytterkture' (449) not only cannot manage the matter he is dealing with but in the end gets himself tangled up in it. Under the protection of metaphor and allegory Parott, however, expresses his indignation at corruption and his frustration at only being able to hurl invective from his place of captivity – even if in a gilded cage – at Wolsey, the person mainly to blame for this state of affairs.

Skelton has much in common with other authors of his time:[5] he bases his works on the classical models of Ovid, Boethius and Chaucer, and he elaborates such themes as the fickleness of Fortune, criticism of contemporary reality and the transference of individual inner conflict and social evils into an allegorical world. He goes back to the form of the dream-vision poem and resorts to the personifications of the morality play which he himself helped to secularize with his *Magnyfycence*. As in Lydgate and especially in Hoccleve, in Skelton's work uncertainty is the dominant note: uncertainty with regard to the fate of society and of the individual, and particularly with regard to the poet's role.

Whereas Hoccleve had divided his *Regement of Princes* into two parts, the mirror of the poet's miserable life and the ideal mirror of the sovereign, Skelton in the *Bowge of Courte* (which may have been a preliminary study for *Magnyfycence*)[6] uses the *speculum* tradition negatively.

4 See for example, among others, M. Evans, *English Poetry in the Sixteenth Century* (London, 1967), p. 59 and S. E. Fish, *John Skelton's Poetry* (New Haven and London, 1965), pp. 55–65.

5 Fish, *Skelton's Poetry*, pp. 55–8.

6 According to L. Winser, '*The Bowge of Courte*: Drama Doubling as Dream', *English Literary Renaissance* 6 (1976) 3–39, the work was conceived not only to be read but

The *Bowge of Courte* opens with a Prologue which narrates a dream the poet had while he was staying at a friend's house in Harwich. In the dream he sees a large ship guided by Fortune and surrounded by a crowd of merchants wishing to go aboard. The owner of the ship, Dame Sans-Pareille, is sitting like a queen, guarded by Danger and Desire. The poet, Drede, wishes to be in the ship, but he is poor and knows no one. Then Desire offers him the talisman Bonne Aventure. Once aboard, Drede notices seven 'persones' who terrify him in several ways despite their feigned indications of friendship. Drede becomes more and more alarmed at some figures behind him. When he hears the word 'murder', he is ready to leap into the sea, but he wakes up and dismisses his dream as a nightmare, although he is aware that sometimes dreams come true. The *Bowge of Courte* is the mirror of the courtiers' wickedness and dishonesty; at the same time it is the mirror of Drede's inability not only to get himself received and accepted at court, but also, as narrator, to learn from his experience as dreamer.

The first four stanzas clearly suggest the idea of uncertainty and instability both as regards the setting of the dream and the nature of the first-person narrator. Indeed, the predominant isotopy is expressed continually and obsessively in the 'mutabylyte' (3) of the Moon,[7] in its 'scorne' (5), in the 'foly and . . . unstedfastnesse' (6) of the human condition, and in the description of Mars preparing for war. The second stanza

> I, callynge to mynde the great auctoryte
> Of poetes olde, whyche, full craftely,
> Under as coverte termes as coude be,
> Can touche a troughte and cloke it subtylly
> Wyth fresshe utteraunce full sentencyously;
> Dyverse in style, some spared not vyce to wrythe,
> Some of moralyte nobly dyde endyte; (8–14)

raises in all its gravity the problem of the loneliness and inability to communicate of the narrator, the 'I', who remains by ellipsis syntacti-

also to be enacted, as various examples of linguistic evidence show, one of them line 534, in which the poet addresses those 'that shall it see or rede'. In the *Bowge* Skelton combines elements taken from theatrical forms like the Disguising, Farce, Morality Play, and Pageant. On the typing of the vices in the morality play, cf. B. Spivack, *Shakespeare and the Allegory of Evil* (New York, 1958), pp. 251ff.

7 On the influence of the moon in dreams, see W. C. Curry, *Chaucer and the Mediaeval Sciences* (London, 1960), pp. 210–11.

cally isolated at the beginning of the line, since with the participle 'callynge to mynde' (8) there is a shift of interest to the authority of the ancient poets, their skill in writing 'of moralyte' (14) and their lasting fame.

The impression of stability only lasts for a moment, however: Ignorance, a character found in morality plays of a humanistic stamp,[8] introduces the commonplace of affected modesty, and this plays its part in eliminating all traces of certainty. He also exhorts the poet to forget his vain hopes of modelling his writings on the ancient poets. Knowing Skelton and the buoyant confidence he had in his skill as a poet, this would seem merely to be a reiterated use of the commonplace. The fourth stanza may, because of its function of *amplificatio* – with proverbs on the impermanence of Fortune,[9] one of the dominant themes – be defined as a bridge passage. After this, however, comes the motif of the narrator's anguish; he falls into a sleep that according to Macrobius' classification is perhaps a 'somnium animale'.[10]

Criticism has often stressed the eccentricity of the ending of the *Bowge of Courte*,[11] so little in keeping with the expectations of readers used to painless awakenings: but the beginning is just as complex and unusual. We may set beside it for comparison the *incipit* of the *Regement of Princes* and that of the *Temple of Glas*:

> Mvsyng vpon the restles bisynesse
> Which that this troubly world hath ay on honde,
> That othir thyng than fruyt of byttirnesse
> Ne yeldeth nought, as I can vndirstonde, (1–4)[12]

[8] See for example *The Nature of the Four Elements* by John Rastell and *Wit and Science* by John Redford.

[9] On the role of Fortune in medieval literature, cf. H. R. Patch, *The Goddess Fortuna in Mediaeval Literature* (Cambridge, Mass., 1927). On the theme of Fortune in the *Bowge of Courte* see J. Scattergood, 'Insecurity in Skelton's *Bowge of Courte*', in P. Boitani and A. Torti, eds., *Genres, Themes and Images in English Literature: From the Fourteenth to the Fifteenth Century* (Tübingen and Cambridge, 1988).

[10] For an analysis of the type of dream the *Bowge of Courte* belongs to, cf. A. C. Spearing, *Medieval Dream-Poetry* (Cambridge, 1976), pp. 197–202, and Heiserman, *Skelton and Satire*, pp. 31–4.

[11] See, among others, Fish, *Skelton's Poetry*, pp. 74–5.

[12] For Hoccleve the edition used is F. J. Furnivall, ed., *Hoccleve's Works: III. The Regement of Princes and Fourteen of Hoccleve's Minor Poems*, EETS ES 72 (London, 1897).

For thouȝt, constreint and greuous heuines,
For pensifhede, and for heiȝ distres,
To bed I went nov þis oþir nyȝt. (1–3)[13]

The cause of Hoccleve's and Lydgate's restless sleep – be it financial problems or a difficult love story – is, so to speak, 'outside' the poet as narrator. While Skelton, on the other hand, makes use of the commonplace of restlessness and anguish, involving even tossing and turning in his sleep, he introduces as the effective cause of his anxiety his inability to write as the 'poetes olde' did (9) and to gain access to the right of immortal 'renome and . . . fame' (15). If we accept Tucker's dating of 1480 for *The Bowge of Courte*,[14] the poem may be taken to reflect, chronologically as well as thematically, Skelton's dissatisfaction with a court that, corrupt though it might be, attracted him, and his awareness of the futility of pursuing the experience of past poets in a language by now sterile. Skelton handles different genres such as dream allegory and *psychomachia*, and uses the topoi of fickle Fortune and of the court as a ship at the mercy of the winds.[15] This treatment of conventional material can be explained by Skelton's intention both to associate himself with the tradition that had grown up from Chaucer through his followers and to show the progressive loss of the values belonging to that tradition.

In the *Bowge of Courte*, the 'prologue' and the 'lytell treatyse' itself reflect the court world in a play of reciprocal mirrorings. The prologue can be divided into two parts: the first presents the waking experience of the narrator in a season that is probably late autumn, while the second is the dream setting proper. Here we find the ship owned by Dame Saunce-Pere, a most beautiful lady seated on a throne draped with precious stuffs and with Daunger and Desyre at her service. Fortune, who is at the ship's helm, is presented in Desyre's words.

13 The *Temple of Glas* quotation comes from J. Norton-Smith, ed., *John Lydgate: Poems* (Oxford, 1966).

14 The suggestion put forward by M. J. Tucker, 'Setting in Skelton's *Bowge of Courte*: A Speculation', *English Language Notes* 7 (1970) 168–75, of an 'early' dating of the work is confirmed, although with a difference of two years (its composition presumably dates from 1482 and not 1480) by F. W. Brownlow, 'The Date of *The Bowge of Courte* and Skelton's Authorship of "A Lamentable of Kyng Edward the IIII" ', *English Language Notes* 22 (1984) 12–20. According to the two critics, on the basis of a Skelton-John Howard association and astronomical data, Skelton's description of court circles refers to the reign of Edward IV and not Henry VII.

15 The theme of the 'ship of fools', apart from appearing in S. Brandt, *Narrenschiff* (1494) and in the Latin version of Locher, *Stultifera Navis* (1497), is already present in Jacquemart Gielé, *Renard le Nouvel* (1288).

As early as the prologue we are given an idea of how the allegorical vision of reality, with the theme of Fortune central to it, has a different meaning that is implied by the very words used by the poet to recount his dream. The reader is aware that the dream experience is circular: when he reaches the end of the poem, therefore, it is natural for him to go back to the beginning and put the opening into its chronological place after the succession of events in the dream. And he thus comes to understand the exact value of terms like 'full craftely' (9), 'coverte termes' (10), 'cloke it subtylly' (11). From the start these are not simple 'innocent' expressions, indicating the allegorical approach of ancient poets, but clear references to the actions of the seven characters Drede is about to meet. The ambiguity of the language is further emphasized by the description of Fortune, to enjoy whose favours Drede must possess '*Bone aventure*' (102). This is tautological, because the expression indicates one of Fortune's aspects. Fortune is not only threatening because of her proverbial changeableness, but also and above all because of the realistic incarnation of her negative qualities in the courtiers that oppose Drede.[16]

The rhetorical subtleties of the ancients, which Drede thought himself capable of equalling at the beginning of the poem, are shown to be ineffective and useless in a world that laughs at his knowledge and where, in Favell's words, 'there were dyverse that sore dyde you manace' (159). The members of this court world maintain the traditional traits of the characters in the *Psychomachia*, but they are locked in double opposition – that of courtiers against Drede and that of courtiers against one another. In this context is it language itself, exploited in all its allusive potential, that is the chosen weapon.[17]

Drede realizes that he is unacceptable at court because of his meagre financial resources, since he is obliged to confess 'I have but smale substaunce' (94). Moreover he is taken unawares and becomes more and more confused when he perceives that words, the tools of trade for a man of letters, are used by the seven characters against him to increase his insecurity to the point of desperation. All of them, in fact, abuse

16 On the Fortune-courtiers relationship see S. J. Kozikowski, 'Allegorical Meanings', pp. 306–7 and also, by the same author, 'Lydgate, Machiavelli and More and Skelton's *Bowge of Courte*', *American Notes and Queries* 15 (1977) 66–7.

17 For an interpretation of Skelton after Bakhtin, see B. Sharratt, 'John Skelton: Finding a Voice – Notes after Bakhtin', in D. Aers, ed., *Medieval Literature. Criticism, Ideology & History* (Brighton, 1986), pp. 192–222; on *The Bowge of Courte* cf. in particular pp. 197–200.

language. Favell 'of wordes . . . had full a poke' (179), and is ready to spew out words of hypocrisy and deceit as the occasion demands. Suspycyon himself is worried about what Favell may have said about him and promises Drede he will entrust important secrets to him, always postponing the actual moment of telling. Even Hervy Hafter advises him not to repeat a single word of his and he and Dysdayne put their heads together to think up a threat that the latter carries out, first by deed and then by word, against Drede, using every means to try to frighten him. And it is Dysdayne who for the first time identifies himself and the others with the court world:

It is greate scorne to see suche a hayne
As thou arte, one that cam but yesterdaye,
With us olde servauntes such maysters to playe. (327–9)

The definition of life at court is then given by Ryote who, introducing an atmosphere of self-indulgence, loose-living and vulgarity, expresses himself as follows: 'This worlde is nothynge but ete, drynke and slepe' (384).

The worst is still to come, however, in the form of the merging of Dysdayne's and Dyssymulation's wickedness, synthesized in this telling image:

But there was poyntynge and noddynge with the hede,
And many wordes sayde in secrete wyse;
They wandred ay and stode styll in no stede. (421–3)

But the two villains do not stop at words spoken in secret, because Dyssymulation carries a knife in one sleeve and a spoonful of honey in the other. On the latter sleeve is written 'A *false abstracte cometh from a fals concrete*' (439). This line, which is often overlooked by critics because it is seen as just a play on words, is instead the starting-point for an approach, if not to *the* meaning, to at least *one* of the meanings of the poem. The sentence rings out as a twofold warning to Drede in his double role of aspiring courtier and poet: the wrong evaluation of concrete reality leads to the formulation of wrong abstractions.

Without going so far as to postulate – as Russell does[18] – a strong nominalistic emphasis in the *Bowge of Courte*, the new epistemological

[18] J. S. Russell, 'Skelton's *Bouge of Court*: A Nominalist Allegory', *Renaissance Papers* (1980) 1–9. Russell considers the problems raised by the *Bowge* as closely

climate introduced by Ockham must have had a more or less direct influence on Skelton, especially if we take into account that of necessity he associated with intellectuals at Cambridge and Oxford.[19]

The sentence written on the sleeve is meant to remind us that abstractions cut off from the concrete reality of an individual should not exist. Drede believed that by using the old allegorical method he could bring a world of shades and abstractions to life again, and that these alluded to the world he was living in. In reality the abstractions have shown themselves in the course of the poem as increasingly concrete and threatening entities (the courtiers themselves who try to bar the poet's reception at court, a reception that is refused to those who wish to 'speak' of such abstractions). It is significant that the philosophical proposition relative to the interdependence of abstract and concrete is pronounced by Dyssymulation, who by his very nature is given to lying. The warnings that this character gives Drede are veritable harbingers of ruin, but they are deceitfully obscure and indirect, for example: 'Ryghte now I spake with one, I trowe, I see –' (458), 'I maye not tell all thynge' (459), and the reference to the mysterious, unknown 'teder man' (484). The latter sums up in his dumb isolation and his threatening unknowableness the negative qualities of the characters that have gradually formed a group round Drede:

> Naye, see where yonder stondeth the teder man!
> A flaterynge knave and false he is, God wote.
> The drevyll stondeth to herken, and he can.
> It were more thryft he boughte him a newe cote;
> It wyll not be, his purse is not on-flote.
> All that he wereth, it is borowed ware;
> His wytte is thynne, his hode is threde-bare. (484–90)

connected to Ockham's nominalist philosophy, and sees the poem as the emblem of the subversion of allegory in the Renaissance.

19 A clear picture of late medieval innovations is offered by G. Leff, *The Dissolution of the Medieval Outlook. An Essay on Intellectual and Spiritual Change in the Fourteenth Century* (New York, 1976). See also by Leff *William of Ockham* (Manchester, 1975). On the various differentiations within Nominalism as a philosophical movement, cf. H. A. Oberman, 'Some Notes on the Theology of Nominalism', *Harvard Theological Review* 53 (1960) 47–76. On the implications of nominalist issues in Chaucer, see the interesting essay by R. A. Peck, 'Chaucer and the Nominalist Questions', *Speculum* 53 (1978) 745–60. On the theory of knowledge in the Middle Ages and on perspective in medieval poetry, cf. respectively: M. L. Colish, *The Mirror of Language. A Study in the Medieval Theory of Knowledge* (Lincoln and London, 1968) and R. A. Peck, 'Public Dreams and Private Myths: Perspective in Middle English Literature', *PMLA* 90 (1975) 461–7.

If we accept the meaning of 'the other man'[20] for the man Dyssymulation refers to, we will understand then how the illusion of being able to use words for the twofold purpose of condemning and being admitted to court now appears as an impossible goal to Drede.

On the realistic plane the 'teder man' in his lack of identity represents what the 'coverte termes' (10) and the 'fresshe utteraunce' (12) of the prologue represent on the allegorical plane in their indefiniteness – the void. Heiserman rightly holds that the 'confusion of the real with the apparent, of the false with the true, of ends and means' can be found in other authors as well, such as John of Salisbury, Walter Map, Langland, Chaucer, Dunbar, Brandt.[21] But in Skelton the result is not so much a sophisticated 'anti-court satire'[22] as an attempt to find his own way of expressing himself. Skelton, spurred on by the need to write, to take 'penne and ynke' (532), recounts his own experience, confused though it be because of the twining of abstract with concrete strands, using a method that is both allegorical and realistic.[23] He does not realize that the fact that the allegorical form is in transformation has made this method more difficult to practise. The contents are no longer the Seven Deadly Sins of traditional homiletics but real court personages who are even allowed to retain their individuality.

An intellectual could not help being influenced by the fact that the certainty of the strict interdependence of language and truth had been undermined, so that he therefore had to come to terms with the ambiguity that had entered into linguistic models.[24] Drede/Skelton learns to his cost that the ability to write, his 'vertu and . . . lytterkture' (449), are not enough to re-create a poem in the manner of the ancient poets,

> . . . the great auctoryte
> Of poetes olde, whyche, full craftely,
> Under as coverte termes as coude be,
> Can touche a troughte and cloke it subtylly
> Wyth fresshe utteraunce full sentencyously. (8–12)

20 On the different possible meanings of the Teder Man, see Winser, 'The Bowge of Courte', pp. 19–24. On the general atmosphere of unease in the *Bowge*, see C. S. Lewis, *English Literature in the Sixteenth Century* (Oxford, 1954), p. 135.

21 Heiserman, *Skelton and Satire*, p. 12.

22 *Ibidem*, p. 65.

23 In his 'Chaucer and the Nominalist Questions', Peck defines the analogous experience of the dreamer in the *Book of the Duchess* by pointing out that no mental construction can be adequate to experience, p. 757.

24 On the impact of Nominalism, see H. W. Boucher, 'Nominalism: The Difference for Chaucer and Boccaccio', *Chaucer Review* 20 (1986) 213–20, especially pp. 214–15.

This is not so much owing to his inadequacy as owing to the differentiation that by now exists between the linguistic realities that are spoken of in the work of art and the objective realities of existing things.[25]

On the one hand the text aims to use allegory to illustrate the evils of humanity personified in courtiers, on the other, it tries to present life at court in a concrete way. The opposition between allegory and mimesis persists right to the end of the poem. The following stanza is particularly significant:

And as he rounded thus in myne ere
Of false collusyon confetryd by assente,
Me thoughte I see lewde felawes here and there
Came for to slee me of mortall entente.
And as they came, the shypborde faste I hente,
And thoughte to lepe; and even with that woke,
Caughte penne and ynke, and wroth this lytell boke.
(526–32)

Disceyte's words 'of false collusyon' (527)[26] confusedly evoke an objective, threatening reality.[27] At the approach of this reality the first-person narrator, Drede, grasps the side of the ship he had boarded at the beginning of the dream, i.e. he takes hold of the Court and at the same time of the *allegory of the Court* (the ship). At this point he jumps down from the ship, thus attempting to abandon the dream object and the means (allegory) used to convey it – which he is now about to use to convey it. It is significant that at this crucial moment he wakes up: Dread gets the better of the dreamer and, with the start typical of dreaming, causes him to wake. The fiction of the dream is thus interrupted, but it is replaced by the poetic re-creation of the dream itself, i.e. by a fiction of a fiction.

25 Peck, 'Chaucer and the Nominalist Questions', p. 760.

26 It must be remembered that one of the characters in *Magnyfycence* is precisely Clokyd Colusyon, who by his own admission has duplicity and falseness as his dominant traits:

Two faces in a hode covertly I bere;
Water in the one hande and fyre in the other.
I can fede forth a fole and lede hym by the eyre;
Falshode in felowshyp is my sworne brother.
By cloked colusyon, I say, and none other,
Comberaunce and trouble in Englande fyrst I began.
From that lorde to that lorde I rode and I ran. (*Magn.*, 710–16)

27 Note the connection between 'false collusyon' and the 'lewde felawes'.

The final stanza summarizes and complicates, in its ambiguity, the subtle and continual effort of interpretation required of the reader:

> I wolde therwith no man were myscontente;
> Besechynge you that shall it see or rede,
> In every poynte to be indyfferente,
> Syth all in substaunce of slumbrynge doth procede.
> I wyll not saye it is mater in dede,
> But yet oftyme suche dremes be founde trewe.
> Now constrewe ye what is the resydewe. (533–9)

By submerging the entire fabric of fiction and the real in sleep ('Sith all in substaunce of slumbrynge doth procede' – 536), the reader is asked to apply impartial and neutral hermeneutics, while there is a simultaneous assertion of the irreality ('I wyll not saye it is mater in dede' – 537) and the truth ('But yet oftyme suche dremes be founde trewe' – 538) of the narrative account, and this is completely open to the same interpretation. There is an implicit effort, therefore, to reconcile the condemnation of the court world as it appears to him in dream and/or reality and his definition of his own worth as a poet, without his running any personal risk.

If the court is characterized by duplicity – an ironic version of Boethius' doctrine of opposites,[28] the poet, who needs that world if he is to live and write, must protect himself by exploiting his literary skill in affirming and at the same time denying what he has written. To prevent anyone being 'myscontente' (533), the reader or the spectator is left free to 'construct' for himself the 'resydewe' (539), the meaning, the *sententia* he prefers, and thus to remain indifferent to the atmosphere of growing fear, especially in the ending.

The motif of doubleness is to be found in the hypothetical reader/spectator whose presence Skelton creates in this poem, since this double figure, who is free to interpret as he chooses, may accept the nightmare as true or reject it as false; or he may – and the poet seems to want to make this clear – evaluate the two categories, falsity/truth as belonging to language, which is increasingly autonomous with respect to the two spheres of reality and truth. Literature is no longer or is not just

[28] Boethius, *De Consolatione Philosophiae* IV, pr. 2. References to the ruling duplicity at court are very frequent: '*Garder le fortune que est mauelz et bone*' – 67; 'That lyned was with doubtfull doublenes' – 178; 'Than, in his hode, I sawe there faces tweyne' – 428.

ethics, and the story Skelton presents to us is not just an exemplary tale,[29] even if at the beginning he tries to follow the path trodden by others with the intention of representing the evil of court life behind the veil of allegory. As the narrative proceeds, the two planes of the *Bowge of Courte*, the literal and the allegorical, merge with each other, and they are often reduced to empty words that allude – not to a higher truth – but to nothingness.

The tentative method of the *Bowge of Courte* is improved on in *Speke Parott*, which is certainly the most complex of Skelton's poems.[30] In *Magnyfycence* Skelton aims at putting the young Henry VIII on his guard against the evils that associating with wicked counsellors can bring in its train, and he exhorts the sovereign to practise the virtues of fortitude and liberality according to the particular tradition of *specula principum*[31] that Lydgate and Hoccleve belong to. In the *Garlande of Laurell*, the mixture of attraction and repulsion inspired in him by the court is a thing of the past and with the confidence given him by his reconciliation with Wolsey, Skelton can give full rein to his self-satisfaction by presenting the reader with his long list of works. Between the above two poems comes *Speke Parott* – chronologically as well as formally – representing an important landmark in Skelton's production. The poem deals with various themes voiced by the bird Parott. He speaks in veiled language against Wolsey. References to the Bible are frequent together with contemporary proverbs. Then a second *persona*, Galathea, comes forth and asks the bird to recite the lament sung by

29 On medieval poetic conception see J. B. Allen, *The Ethical Poetic of the Later Middle Ages: A decorum of convenient distinction* (Toronto, Buffalo, London, 1982).

30 Cf. P. Green, *John Skelton* (London, 1978), p. 29 and A. C. Spearing, *Medieval to Renaissance in English Poetry* (Cambridge, 1985), p. 265, which offers a clear exposition of the problems raised by *Speke Parott*, pp. 265–77, and to which the present analysis is indebted. For a detailed examination of Biblical and literary references in general, see H. L. R. Edwards, *Skelton. The Life and Times of an Early Tudor Poet* (London, 1949), pp. 182–99. On the structure of *Speke Parott*, cf. J. Holloway, *The Charted Mirror: Literary and Critical Essays* (London, 1960), pp. 21–2.

31 Skelton was tutor to Prince Arthur and probably later on to the young Henry, and it was for them that he wrote a *Speculum Principis*, edited by F. M. Salter, 'Skelton's *Speculum Principis*', *Speculum* 9 (1934) 25–37. On Skelton's position at court see, among others, R. F. Green, *Poets and Princepleasers: Literature and the English Court in the Late Middle Ages* (Toronto, 1980), pp. 76–9 and 193–4, and G. Kipling, 'Henry VII and the Origins of Tudor Patronage', in G. F. Lytle and S. Orgel, eds., *Patronage in the Renaissance* (Princeton, 1981), pp. 117–64, especially pp. 128–33, in which the intensity of cultural exchange between English intellectuals and the Franco-Burgundian men of letters present at court is given particular attention.

Pamphilus. Several envoys follow, in which Parott condemns Wolsey's policy at Calais and his own ignorant detractors who do not understand his language. At the end of the poem the bird bursts into general satire. His lament for the time is a lament for all times, thus emphasizing the difficulties inherent in the struggle against evil.

A number of critics have stressed how difficult it is to grasp the meaning of *Speke Parott*, which P. Green defines as 'an enigma, a nightmare, a nest of bewildering ambiguities'.[32] Parott, a bird of Paradise from exotic climes, able to quote the Bible for his own ends, skilled in the use of the most diverse tongues, a lover of mirrors, is undoubtedly a many-sided character – and Skelton seems to want to invest his *persona* with a series of contradictory meanings. In spite of the various interpretations put forward with regard to Parott as a character,[33] and with respect to the structure[34] and the satirical background to the poem, the meaning of *Speke Parott* remains obscure.[35] Almost every line has been subjected to careful examination and the various sources and analogues have been minutely analysed; but the basic ambiguity remains – and perhaps this is Skelton's message. We have already noted that language plays a very important role in the *Bowge of Courte* in overlapping in various ways the literal and allegorical planes and in creating an atmosphere of real menace for Drede; in *Speke Parott*, the language *is* the protagonist, the focal point of a narrative that discusses itself and its theoretical premises.

I shall not enter into the vexed question of the dating of *Speke Parott*, since others have made their contributions to this.[36] I agree with Edwards, however, when he states that Skelton is ready in this work to exploit the potentialities of language and of poetic communication to represent, in the person of Parott, the poetic gift itself.[37] The fragmentary nature of the text,[38] the multiplication of the Envoys, the appearance of the mysterious Galathea, the presence within the one poem of different genres, from satire to elegy, with the juxtaposition of Biblical passages to be interpreted according to their typology and of overt at-

32 Green, *John Skelton*, p. 29.
33 Cf. D. Lawton, 'Skelton's Use of *Persona*', *Essays in Criticism* 30 (1980) 9–28, which examines Skelton's most important poems. On *Speke Parott*, pp. 19–27.
34 Cf. F. W. Brownlow, 'The Boke Compiled by Maister Skelton, Poet Laureate, Called Speake Parrot', *English Literary Renaissance* 1 (1971) 3–26.
35 Cf. Heiserman, *Skelton and Satire*, pp. 141–5 and N. O. Wallace, 'The Responsibilities of Madness: John Skelton, "Speke, Parrot", and Homeopathic Satire', *Studies in Philology* 82 (1985) 60–80.
36 On the dating cf. W. Nelson, *John Skelton. Laureate* (New York, 1939), pp. 158–84.
37 Edwards, *Skelton*, p. 191.
38 Cf. Nelson, *John Skelton*, pp. 158–84.

tacks on Wolsey and his politics, are all elements that make this a difficult poem to approach. Yet Skelton offers us a complicated but fascinating key to an understanding of the work, as long as we agree to do as Parott does, and look through the mirror – a metaphor for the poet and poetry, while poetry, in its turn, is a metaphor for the contemporary, contingent world, but also for the domain of the eternal.

From the very beginning the mirror appears as a complex, polysemic metaphor: in his cage, the parrot has 'A myrrour of glasse, that I may tote therin' (10) and since he is inside the cage, Parott can see the world in the mirror. The cage may allude to court favour as a form of gilded prison: the location of the cage is in fact with 'greate ladyes of estate' (6); it is the gathering-place of delightful maidens who joke and play with Parott, and in it the mirror reflects its surroundings – the court. Later on the parrot adds further information about the value of the mirror:

> The myrrour that I tote in, *quasi diaphonum*,
> *Vel quasi speculum, in enigmate*,
> *Elencticum*, or ells *enthimematicum*. (190–2)

With Parott's speeches Skelton offers us a series of possibilities for the interpretation not only of this poem but of all his poetry; Parott is the poet who, despite his God-given inspiration,[39] can only partly make his prophecy, because, in accordance with I Corinthians 13: 12 man on earth is enshrouded in darkness. The confusion that derives from Parott's clouded vision is '*Confuse distrybutyve*' (198); it is orderly, containing the possibility of being understood by whoever wants to understand it. Parott still has to defend himself by means of '*metaphora, alegoria*' (202), so as not to be condemned on account of the truths he first tries to communicate to the maidens, then to Galathea and lastly to his readers. But it is clear that, given the polysemic weight of the mirror metaphor, this is only one of the planes on which it can be read. To take the quotation from I Corinthians fully into account, we must observe that the passage paraphrased by Parott is followed by a long discussion of prophecy (I Cor. 14: 1–25) dealing specifically with the difference between the gift of tongues and that of prophecy, and leading up to Paul's

[39] As Brownlow, 'The Boke Compiled', p. 8, n. 16, notes, Parott's reference to Melpomene alludes to poetry's power to cause its listeners to fall 'in a softe slepe of contemplatyf delectacion' (Skelton, *Bibliotheca Historica of Diodorus Siculus*, eds. F. M. Salter and H. L. R. Edwards, EETS 233 – London, 1956 for 1950, p. 359).

condemnation of the deliberate obscurity of language: 'Ita et vos per linguam nisi manifestum sermonem dederitis: quomodo scietur id quod dicitur? eritis enim in aera loquentes' (So likewise you, except you utter by the tongue plain speech, how shall it be known what is said? For you shall be speaking into the air; I Cor. 14: 9). The Apostle then adds: 'Et ideo qui loquitur lingua, oret ut interpretetur' (And therefore he that speaketh by a tongue, let him pray that he may interpret; I Cor. 14: 13).[40]

On his own admission Parott seems to have something of both tendencies in him: he is pure breath, pure sound, a mere relayer, on the one hand; on the other he is a special bird, the offspring of Deucalion, bird-man, and bird of Paradise that 'dothe not putrefy' (213) – poetry as truth. If we take into account and accept this antinomy, we understand the originality of a poem that, more explicitly than the rest of Skelton's works, offers us a synthesis of his experiments in combining and/or transcending tradition and innovation in the field of poetic expression.

Speke Parott can be read in various ways. In the allegory the reader, and especially the reader of Skelton's times, accustomed as he was to uncovering other meanings behind the literal one, clearly recognizes Wolsey as the target for Skelton's satire. Parott's polyglot jargon and the reference to the Grammarians' War are directed at Wolsey and his intense activity both in international affairs and in the field of education.[41] Thus the complex typological allusions to Wolsey made by mentioning Aaron (59) and Melchizedek (60) and other Biblical figures and events, with reference to the contemporary political situation (64–7), and the use made of the languages of the countries – France, Spain, and Flanders – where Wolsey was actively negotiating at the time, open up one plane of interpretation.

As we have already clearly seen, the poem is not a unified whole; it is divided into different, apparently unconnected, parts: Parott's poem, with the appearance of Galathea, the four *Envoys* and the *Laucture de Parott*. Again, Parott's poem can be subdivided into: (a) introduction of the speaker, (b) attack on Wolsey by means of Biblical episodes, (c) assumption of attitude towards the Grammarians' War and (d) a ballad dedicated to Galathea taken from a popular love poem. There is no

40 On the prophecy/gift of tongues relationship, cf. N. Frye, *The Great Code* (London, Melbourne, Henley, 1982), p. 127 and p. 219. On the way I Corinthians is used in *Speke Parott*, see Fish, *Skelton's Poetry*, pp. 152–7; the analysis of the poem is particularly interesting from the point of view of style (pp. 135–76).

41 Cf. Spearing, *Medieval to Renaissance*, pp. 273–5.

doubt that the most interesting part is lines 141–232 (part c). First Parott enters into the controversy about the teaching of Greek, since Skelton had sided with the 'Trojans' in the diatribes between these and the 'Greeks', not so much because he was against Greek as because he was against the method used to teach it at Cambridge and Oxford.[42] There is perhaps also a brief polemical reference to Erasmus' translation of the New Testament: 'For ye scrape out good scrypture, and set in a gall: / Ye go about to amende, and ye mare all' (153–4). Parott expresses his concern as to 'How the rest of good lernyng is roufled up and trold' (168), because Greek is about to oust Latin and the argumentations of Scholastic philosophy, to the extent of relegating the liberal arts to a sphere of secondary importance; he then comes to grips with the arguments central to the Grammarians' War. Parott, Skelton's mouthpiece, denounces the rejection of the traditional method of teaching Latin and the resulting neglect of basic grammatical texts, like Donatus' and Priscian's; and he insists that classical writers should be approached by normative means rather than by the direct method of imitation.

The two stanzas that follow are Parott's self-defence of his way of speaking:

> The myrrour that I tote in, *quase diaphonum*,
> *Vel quasi speculum, in enigmate*,
> *Elencticum*, or ells *enthimematicum*,
> For logicions to loke on, somwhat *sophistice*;
> Retoricyons and oratours in freshe humanyte,
> Support Parrot, I pray you, with your suffrage ornate,
> Of *confuse tantum* avoydynge the chekmate.
>
> But of that supposicyon that callyd is arte,
> *Confuse distrybutyve*, as Parrot hath devysed,
> Let every man after his merit take his parte;
> For in this processe, Parrot nothing hath surmysed,
> No matter pretendyd, nor nothyng enterprysed,
> But that *metaphora, alegoria* withall,
> Shall be his protectyon, his pavys and his wall. (190–203)

His obscure form of speech is deliberate, in that it serves to protect him from any attack that might be made on him by Wolsey, and it is at the

42 On the so-called Grammarians' War and on the polemics regarding the teaching of languages, cf. Nelson, *John Skelton*, pp. 148–57. On Humanism in England, cf. R. Weiss, *Humanism in England During the Fifteenth Century* (Oxford, 1967).

same time the consequence of the literary tradition that Skelton inherits from the past. The *metaphora* and the *alegoria* that Parott hides behind are no different from the 'coverte termes' of the *Bowge of Courte*.

Skelton has a much more ambitious programme here, however. He intends to exploit the Pauline metaphor of the mirror and that of the gift of tongues to communicate to his readers the difficulties and dangers of writing at court – or just writing in general. Indeed, even if the poet makes overt reference only to the metaphor of the mirror, the presence of the parrot openly characterized by notable multilingualism and by the gift of prophecy automatically sends the reader back to Chapter 14 of I Corinthians and to the distinction between language and prophecy mentioned above. Parott's knowledge can only be obscure and his vision indirect because he is on earth and shut in the cage that is the court. What he has said and what he will say is confused, *confuse tantum*, but also *confuse distrybutyve*, a confusion that can be made orderly by poetry ('arte' – 197) to a degree corresponding to the ability of the listener or reader to interpret correctly. Parott would seem to speak in two ways: he possesses the gift of tongues – to use Paul's definition – in that he is capable of emitting various sounds in 'Latyn, Ebrue, Caldee, Greke, Frenshe, Dowche, Spaynyshe', and also of imitating the sounds made by animals, and he shows himself to be a prophet in asking to be listened to and understood: 'Make moche of Parrot, the pogegay ryall' (217). By attributing to Parott's *persona* qualities and functions which are often contradictory on a literal level, Skelton tries to exploit to the utmost the metaphorical possibilities of this prosopopoeia. To go back to the Epistle to the Corinthians, Paul's exhortation to them to make use of all means of communication yields a significant analogy with Parott's method of recounting reality; Paul says: 'Cum convenitis, unusquisque vestrum psalmum habet, doctrinam habet, apocalypsim habet, linguam habet, interpretationem habet: omnia ad aedificationem fiant' (When you come together, every one of you hath a psalm, hath a doctrine, hath a revelation, hath a tongue, hath an interpretation: let all things be done to edification; I Cor. 14: 26). And in the course of the poem Parott makes reference to the Psalms, makes a great show of his ability to quote the Bible and of his knowledge of languages and, finally, offers the reader an apocalyptic vision of the contemporary world in the *Laucture*.

Syntagmatically, then, the poem has a linear movement as an amalgam of various compositions attributable to different literary genres, from the narrator/protagonist's presentation of himself to the final picture of the miserable condition England had been brought to by Wolsey.

Paradigmatically the poem functions as a progressive, even though insufficient, clarification, by means of a complex selection of Biblical episodes, both historical and apocalyptic, of the basic theme of the work, which is the conflict between the traditional and right way (according to Skelton) of wielding authority in all fields and in all forms, and the new high-handed way of doing so. If 'In mesure is tresure, *cum sensu maturato: / Ne tropo sanno, ne tropo mato*' (62–3), then Wolsey's exceeding his office and the sovereign's allowing his authority to be usurped are both to be condemned in the name of equipoise and moderation, virtues Skelton had already praised in *Magnyfycence*. The politics of self-aggrandizement attributed to Wolsey[43] had caused many ills and the weakening of the country.

To attack Wolsey[44] and get away with it, Parott uses parables:

> For trowthe in parabyll ye wantonlye pronounce,
> Langagys divers; yet undyr that dothe reste
> Maters more precious than the ryche jacounce. (364–6)

His way of expressing himself can have two consequences: Parott's talk can be considered absolute nonsense by those who do not understand (by those who do not share Skelton's alarm); or his parables may make hard reading, the allusions becoming clear only after the elements of comparison have been found in the texts from which the parables have been taken. As far as the question of the folly of Parott – and of the world in general – is concerned,[45] this – together with the question of wisdom – is posed from the very beginning: indeed Parott is foolish and wise at the same time. 'Phronessys for frenessys may not hold her way' (47), but only because of people who refuse to grasp the meaning hidden in the parrot's words. The gift of tongues, 'To lerne all langage and hyt to speke aptlye' (45), may be judged as madness if the person the message is addressed to is not an 'initiate', if he has no code in common with the

43 See the episode (309–12) of the Great Seal that Wolsey took with him to Calais, thus causing considerable administrative problems.

44 Skelton's hatred of Wolsey is, however, excessive if the role he did indeed play as patron of the arts is taken into account. Cf. in this regard W. G. Zeeveld, *Foundations of Tudor Policy* (Cambridge, Mass., 1948), pp. 18–26 and 57ff.; Zeeveld examines the close relationship between culture and the sovereign in the early Tudor period. On Wolsey's patronage see J. K. McConica, *English Humanists and Reformation Politics under Henry VIII and Edward VI* (Oxford, 1968), pp. 8, 54, 58, 63, 70, 122, 270.

45 On Parott's madness, cf. Wallace, 'The Responsibilities of Madness', pp. 74ff. On inspired frenzy, like Parott's *divinus furor*, see M. West, 'Skelton and the Renaissance Theme of Folly', *Philological Quarterly* 50 (1971) 23–35, pp. 34–5.

utterer of the message. Failure to understand the message is a likely outcome of reading if the poet's criticism of the exponents of the New Learning is well grounded. They are slated with being too ready to deviate from the norm and with having created a scandalous situation: 'Set *Sophia* asyde, for every Jack Raker / And every mad medler must now be a maker' (160–1).

To solve the enigma of Parott's apparent madness we need to examine the *Envoys*. In *Lenvoy primere* Parott who represents the *signifier* (the indistinct phonemes of his rigmarole) and the *signified* (the 'parabyll' derived from the Bible) is identified with the message itself, 'Go, litelle quayre, namyd the Popagay' (278). Narrator and narrative are one and the same. Only madmen can think that 'ye arre furnysshyd with knakkes, / That hang togedyr as fethyrs in the wynde' (292–3). Indeed 'whoo lokythe wyselye in your warkys may fynde / Muche frutefull mater' (296–7). In the *Secunde Lenvoy* the idea is renewed that 'nodypollys and gramatolys of smalle intellygens' (318) will deny the value of the poem, or rather of the 'poemys' (316). The use of the plural form, like 'warkys' (296) a few lines before, allows the poet to be lexically identified with Parott by means of his works. In a situation of total ignorance, due to the new educational ideas that the 'new men' have introduced into the schools and universities ('To rude ys there reason to reche to your sentence' – 319), the message will not be shared.

Parott's 'natural' folly is contrasted with the 'artificial' folly of Wolsey, who is never mentioned directly but is always there by allusion.[46] Wolsey's conduct is such as to seem against all reason and completely mad: 'To suche thynges ympossybyll, reason cannot consente; / Muche money, men sey, there madly he hathe spente' (334–5), and such as to involve the whole country: 'Frantiknes dothe rule and all thyng commaunde; / Wylfulnes and Braynles now rule all the raye' (420–1). Parott's 'good' craziness is hard to interpret, because the deliberate obscurity of the allegory makes its meaning hard to decipher; Wolsey's 'evil' senselessness is at times quite open and evident, but in the long run it is identified with the general complaint about the ills of the time, a stereotyped genre of wide circulation and as such involving little risk. When the attack would appear to be coming out into the open, it takes cover behind the commonplace, which is reassuring and protective.

46 The distinction between 'natural' and 'artificial' folly is introduced by R. L. Ramsay, ed., *Magnyfycence* by John Skelton, EETS ES 98 (London, 1908), pp. xcvii ff., which contrasts Fancy with Folly; Fancy is represented as whimsical and simple, whereas Folly actively incarnates the principle of sin.

Parott, apart from his gift of the gab, his double-talk and repetition of what others say – and hence what the poet says – also has the gift of the teacher who, if only obscurely, can point to some of the problems then afflicting England. To do this a new dialogic relationship is established between Parott and Galathea, a character who appears unexpectedly on the scene. There have been various critical interpretations of Galathea.[47] Lawton's suggestion[48] that she is an 'open *persona*' with the function of making the meaning of the poem clear in her verbal exchanges with Parott, is the most valid. It confirms the need Skelton felt to introduce the imaginary audience into the poem, the audience that could construct, as happens at the end of the *Bowge*, the sense of the message. Galathea refers us back, of course, to the nymph beloved of the Cyclops[49] but above all, as the marginal gloss shows,[50] to the early twelfth-century Latin comedy *Pamphilus*, which had such a wide circulation in England that it had been raised to the height of *auctoritas* by the middle of the same century.[51] Just as in *Pamphilus* the love story between Pamphilus and Galathea develops by means of a series of dialogues between the two and between the characters and the *anus*,[52] so in Skelton's poem Galathea's function consists in solving, even if only partially, through dialogue with Parott, the enigma of what the parrot has said up to that point. And the *enigma* is not to be understood purely in the Pauline sense of limited human knowledge against the total, complete knowledge of the hereafter, but also as a rhetorical figure. It is to be understood as a self-contained allegory, whose basic idea can be grasped, even though with difficulty, if the social and psychological situations of the speaker are known in precise detail.[53] Parott's talk can be considered an enigma, in that it is in a still less accessible form than

47 On the meaning of Galathea, cf. Wallace, 'The Responsibilities of Madness', pp. 74–6; Edwards, *Skelton*, pp. 191–9; Spearing, *Medieval to Renaissance*, pp. 272–3.

48 Lawton, 'Skelton's Use of *Persona*', p. 27.

49 Ovid, *Metamorphoses* XIII, ll. 737–899.

50 'Hic occurrat memorie Pamphilus de Amore Galathee' (Scattergood, *John Skelton*, p. 460).

51 On *Pamphilus* and on its influence on European literature in general, see S. Pittaluga, *Commedie latine del XII e del XIII secolo*, III (Genova, Istituto di Filologia classica e medievale, 1980) 11–137, especially pp. 13–18 and 41–4; on the early dating of the work, see P. Dronke, 'A Note on *Pamphilus*', *Journal of the Warburg and Courtauld Institutes* 42 (1979) 225–30.

52 On the structure of *Pamphilus*, see P. Dronke, 'Narrative and Dialogue in Medieval Secular Drama', in P. Boitani and A. Torti, eds., *Literature in Fourteenth-Century England* (Tübingen and Cambridge, 1983), pp. 99–120.

53 For the definition of enigma, cf. H. Lausberg, *Handbuch der literarischen Rhetorik* (München, 1960), It. trans. *Elementi di retorica* (Bologna, 1969), p. 235.

metaphora; it is *alegoria*, and a way to get to the bottom of it is suggested by the few lines given to Galathea.[54]

If we agree with Skelton's position, according to which 'arte' is 'supposicyon' (197), we can then apply to art what nominalistic logic predicates of *suppositio* – of the denotative meaning of the terms found in the proposition. In this sense, because *suppositio* is a sign's 'standing for' something else,[55] what Parott says may be read as standing for something else, as a '*metaphora, alegoria* withall' (202) behind which various meanings are concealed. The suppositious relationship that exists in art between the sign and what it refers to requires an interpretative elaboration that does not give one answer only, but several, according to the various levels of participation. As Parott says: 'Let every man after his merit take his parte' (199). Only very few men, and these only by strenuous effort, are able to understand the message.

Up until Galathea's appearance, Parott has spoken in an obscure, sibylline way, using ambiguous rhetorical figures like the *elenchus* and the *enthymeme* that logicians, suspecting Sophistic implications, are wary of. In his arguing Parott has used premises without reaching any conclusion, or he has even skipped a premise. In lines 113–23, for example, there are references to Biblical episodes taken from Jeremiah, Exodus, Judges and Psalms, and a possible association among them and with Wolsey comes from the fact that all the persons spoken of, even though they lived in different periods, were enemies of Israel that no one stood up against because all of Israel's champions were dead. The following lines (124–30) deal with a personal problem of Skelton's, in that they allude to Wolsey's intention to change the laws governing sanctuaries, and Skelton, as we know, lived in the sanctuary of Westminster.

54 L. Ebin, 'Poetics and Style in Late Medieval Literature', in L. Ebin, ed., *Vernacular Poetics in the Middle Ages*, Studies in Medieval Culture XVI (Kalamazoo, Michigan, 1984), pp. 263–93, especially pp. 283–93, points out the transformation in the relationship between poetry and style evident in Skelton's and Stephen Hawes' works. Hawes manipulates various stylistic forms in his later works in order to create a sense of obscurity and mystery in line with his conception of the poem as prophecy. According to Ebin, Skelton too passes from the utmost dissatisfaction with the traditional style in the *Bowge of Courte* to the clear expression of his dilemma between past and present in *Speke Parott*. Here Parott tries out various stylistic possibilities without finding complete satisfaction in any of them until he reaches the 'clear, unadorned and vigorous medium of the concluding stanzas' (p. 287). It is my opinion that the expressive tension in Skelton is never relieved, not even at the end, which is not so much an innovation as a return to the commonplace of the complaint.

55 The term *suppositio* must be understood, especially after the fourteenth century, in the sense of nominalist logic. See Peter of Spain's *Summulae Logicales* 6.03 and Ockham's *Summa Logicae* I, 63.

Even if his way of doing so is indirect, the poet's intention to draw a parallel between Biblical episodes and contemporary history is clear. Skelton followed this procedure throughout the first part of *Speke Parott* but he then gradually gave it up, because it could cause confusion and could thus make interpretation impossible.

The invitation extended to the rhetoricians and orators to support Parott with their 'suffrage ornate' (195) so as to avoid utter confusion appears like an attempt to exploit the very means used by the proponents of the New Learning with the aim of showing how the unconventional use of language can be extremely dangerous and sterile. Shortly before (141–82) Parott had illustrated the negative consequences and the unreasonableness of the new approach to languages in contrast with the traditional Scholastic method. Parott, like some rhetoricians and orators, expresses himself in figures that the logicians considered not entirely orthodox; the clear distinction postulated between *confuse tantum* and *confuse distrybutyve* shows that the method of communicating by obscure allusions is no longer seen as correct, because there is the danger of its creating ambiguous associations between the object of the satire and the satirist. To avoid this danger Skelton introduces into the poem – which was certainly written over a considerable period of time – the *persona* of Galathea, whose appearance (on stage?) is immediately preceded by the admonition '*Candidi lectores, callide callete, vestrum fovete Psitacum, etc.*' (232 b). The identification of Pamphilus' complaint with a pious allegory that sees Christ in Pamphilus (meaning 'all-lover') and humanity in Besse,[56] limits the sense of the passage to the purely moral plane, and the multiplicity of allusions, for which the following *Envoys* again provide the substratum, is lost. It is true that Galathea exhorts Parott to get rid of his various sophisms – 'Nowe, Parott, my swete byrde, speke owte yet ons agayn, / Sette asyde all sophysms, and speke now trew and playne.' (447–8) – and that she urges him to utter a long tirade against the ills of the time. It should be pointed out, however, that paradoxically, from the point of view of the satire, the last part of the *complaint* is less clear, because it is vaguer, more stereotyped, more in line with the tradition of admonitions to the sovereign. In *Lenvoy royall* Parott takes up the allusion to *Pamphilus* again and invites the poem, which has become identified with the name of Parott, to 'Go, propyr Parotte, my popagay, / That lordes and ladies thys pamflett may behold, / With notable clerkes' (357–9). For an attempt to

56 Edwards, *Skelton*, p. 193.

establish Galathea's identity, the use of the word 'pamflett', taken from the same play and having the same meaning of brief literary composition, is interesting, as is the choice of the verb 'behold', which would seem to imply, as we have seen in the *Bowge of Courte*,[57] a likely theatrical performance of the work. Indeed the dramatic way Parott presents himself – 'My name ys Parott, a byrde of Paradyse, / By Nature devysed of a wonderowus kynde, / Deyntely dyetyd with dyvers delycate spyce' (1–3), the use of the deictic, exophoric, 'These maydens' (11), the request for food 'Now a nutmeg, a nutmeg, *cum gariopholo*' (183), and the interlocutory function of Galathea – all these elements, added to Skelton's theatrical competence, make us think of a dramatic substratum to the poem. But this is just *one* of the possible readings, and just as Galathea, within the text, represents the participating reader that asks Parott for explanations, so the reader and/or spectator is called on to do his share in clarifying the obscurity that reigns in the work: 'Thus myche Parott hathe opynlye expreste; / Let se who dare make up the reste' (381–2). In a different setting, what is required of the reader is analogous to what is required of him in the *Bowge of Courte*: 'Now constrewe ye what is the resydewe' (539).

It can be stated in conclusion that Skelton in *Speke Parott*, as in *The Bowge of Courte*, more or less consciously intends to stress the sense of uncertainty typical of a period of transition from the Middle Ages to the Renaissance, of the passage from medieval literary models to more typically Renaissance ones.[58] Skelton's response to this difficulty is such that his works show us not only his interest in the new – the study of languages, especially Greek, and his desire to ensure himself lasting fame[59] – but also his ties with the poets of the past, whose worthy disciple he considers himself to be, and with their metaphorical and allegorical methods.

Let us now go back to the key image in *Speke Parott* – the mirror as metaphor of language and reality. Parott's mirror has a double function, passive and active, as does a material mirror: it gives a reflection in so far as it represents the original in all its parts, while it is also an image because it offers something new and distinct from the original, with the loss of certain characteristics of the original such as its physical dimen-

57 Cf. note 6.

58 S. Medcalf, 'On Reading Books from an half-alien culture', in Medcalf, *The Later Middle Ages*, pp. 1–55, especially pp. 45–6.

59 On Skelton's full awareness of his own value as a poet, see R. Skelton, 'The Master Poet: John Skelton as Conscious Craftsman', *Mosaic* 6 (1973) 67–92.

sions.[60] In this sense *Speke Parott* is a mimetic representation of contemporary society, with its disorder, confusion and uncertainty about the great political issues and with regard to culture; yet it cannot help but constitute as well an image of a reality – specific, shattered, deconstructed – in which every constituent element helps to form something profoundly different from that reality. At times the language too reproduces a sense of deconstruction, cutting itself loose from the relationship of *adaequatio* to the reality it represents and degrading itself to mere sounds and incomprehensible sound sequences, as in the attempt to reproduce the parrot's rigmarole:

> 'But ware the cat, Parot, ware the fals cat!'
> With, 'Who is there? A mayd?' Nay, nay, I trow!
> Ware, ryat, Parrot, ware ryot, ware that!
> 'Mete, mete, for Parrot, mete I say, how!'
> Thus dyvers of language by lernyng I grow:
> With, 'Bas me, swete Parrot, bas me, swete swete;'
> To dwell amonge ladyes, Parrot, is mete. (99–105)

or in the reply to Galathea, characterized by the build-up of words that clinch the condemnation of Wolsey's excesses:

> To jumbyll, to stombyll, to tumbyll down lyke folys;
> To lowre, to droupe, to knele, to stowpe and to play
> cowche-quale;
> To fysshe afore the nette and to drawe polys.
> He maketh them to bere babylles, and to bere a lowe sayle;
> He caryeth a kyng in hys sleve, yf all the worlde fayle;
> He facithe owte at a flusshe with, 'Shewe, take all!'
> Of Pope Julius cardys, he ys chefe Cardynall. (425–31)

Allegory in the *Bowge of Courte* is a pre-text for representing the dangerousness of court life, but it is also a con-text in which the problematic nature of a new interaction between consciousness and abstraction is delineated.[61] In *Speke Parott*, allegory is by Parott's definition 'his protectyon, his pavys and his wall' (203), that is, a veiled, enigmatic way of comprising the whole of reality, the reality of England's condition – of

60 On the imagery of the mirror in medieval and Renaissance literature, cf. Introduction.
61 Cf. Russell, 'Skelton's *Bouge of Court*', especially pp. 4–6.

the senseless behaviour of men and of Wolsey in particular, and of the frenzy of Parott-poet, who aims at presenting a satirical meditation that is almost a political pamphlet (a predominant form from the end of the sixteenth century onwards).[62] On looking in the Pauline *speculum*, however, he finds himself also having to come to terms for a moment with his identity as poet-prophet, who with God's inspiration must correct men and himself, because he too is a man.

Despite their thematic similarity, the difference between the *Bowge of Courte* and *Speke Parott* is quite clear. In the former poem the allegorical approach is such that Drede *suffers* the transformation of the allegory and does not take into account that at the basis of knowledge lies the observation of phenomena and that reality is therefore vigorous and compelling by comparison with abstraction; in the latter poem Parott, by centring so many meanings on himself, is the subject and object of the narration. He is its *subject* in that his purpose, notwithstanding his deliberate obscurity, is to teach and present a mirror-image of the reality of the age; and its *object* in so far as Parott himself, with his imitation of language-sounds and the crazy behaviour of men, feels he shares in the world's folly, if only to show it up the more clearly.[63] *Speke Parott*'s innovation compared with the *Bowge of Courte* is thus above all formal. The allegory in the *Bowge of Courte* is more metaphorical in the sense that the characters have a tendency towards abstraction, whereas the allegory in *Speke Parott* is more metonymical, since Parott/Narrator does not represent a quality incarnate in a person but a series of Biblical and contemporary figures and events. Some of these, by being located contiguously in the poem, allude to real persons, and ultimately to one real personage, Wolsey.[64] And it is precisely in *Speke Parott* that Skelton, by his own admission working within the canons of allegory – or even more precisely of Biblical typology, to the extent of making Wolsey out to be a kind of Antichrist[65] – is more innovative, because he makes use of

62 For the use of the mirror metaphor in satire, see Grabes, *The Mutable Glass*, pp. 99–103.

63 On the homeopathic function of folly, cf. again Wallace, 'The Responsibilities of Madness', especially pp. 78–80.

64 On metaphorical and non-metaphorical (metonymic) allegory see the interesting essay by H. W. Boucher, 'Metonymy in Typology and Allegory, with a Consideration of Dante's *Comedy*', in M. W. Bloomfield, ed., *Allegory, Myth, and Symbol*, Harvard English Studies 9 (Cambridge, Mass., London, 1981), pp. 129–45, which contains a careful analysis of the question.

65 Cf. ll. 444–5: 'Ryn God, rynne Devyll! Yet the date of Owur Lord / And the date of the Devyll dothe shurewlye accord', where the proverbial expression alludes to Wolsey and his usurpation of authority.

allegory not as simple recovery of a medieval tradition but as a means whose potentialities he exploits to transmit his vision of a confused, disorderly, crazy world. It is the function of poetry, however, to show the de-composition of this vision and to re-compose it, even if differently, just as the mirror does with the reflected image. The reader is called on to participate in this work of re-composition – that is, of interpretation of a multiform reality that eludes definition and of a language that is often inadequate to this task.

In the *persona* of Parott, Skelton succeeds in activating three planes pertinent to a literary text: the rhetorical (or plane of persuasion); the poetic (or mimesis of the *imaginaire*); the hermeneutic (or plane of interpretation). Parott is a *laudator temporis acti* and Wolsey's implacable accuser; he uses language to imitate the reality that surrounds him and, divinely-inspired *persona* that he is, he succeeds in transferring reality into the text in the form of metaphor – metaphor open to interpretation even though this involves the utmost difficulty. In the multiplicity of functions he performs, Parott is therefore the epitome of Skelton's comprehensive, multiform conception of poetry.

INDEX